THE POLISH QUESTION

IN THE RUSSIAN STATE DUMA

THE POLISH QUESTION

IN THE RUSSIAN STATE DUMA

EDWARD CHMIELEWSKI

THE UNIVERSITY OF TENNESSEE PRESS : KNOXVILLE

LIBRARY OF CONGRESS CATALOG NUMBER 77–100411
STANDARD BOOK NUMBER 87049–110–5

Copyright © 1970 by The University of Tennessee Press, Knoxville
Manufactured in the United States of America

PREFACE

WHILE AN INCREASING AMOUNT of scholarship has been devoted to the constitutional period of Russian history, 1905–1917, many lacunae remain. Indeed, some of the principal historical problems of the period have been treated only marginally. Certainly the issue of nationalism must be studied as one of the keys to a fuller understanding of the last years of the multinational Russian Empire. After 1905, the Polish question, always the most critical minority question faced by Russia after the partitions of Poland at the end of the eighteenth century, proved to be a particularly sensitive touchstone of Russian opinion, both in the government and in the newly created legislature. Russian approaches to the Polish problem during the constitutional period throw light not only on Russo-Polish relations but also on the more general question of Russian nationalism and its impact on the fate of the Russian Empire.

This study is intended to view the Polish question in the Russian State Duma as a critical aspect of Russian domestic history and the constitutional experiment of the early twentieth century. Apart from the intrinsic historical significance of the Polish question, its handling by the Russian government relates to the entire spectrum of problems faced by Russia at the time—the viability of Russian liberalism, the adaptability of the government to changing political conditions, the dangers involved in a possible war hastened by nationalism, and, of course, the ultimate failure of the reform movement and the oncoming of the revolutions of 1917.

This book is based heavily on the stenographic reports of the State Duma and the State Council. Contemporary newspapers, periodicals, and memoirs have also been used. There have been several recent contributions to the subject by Soviet and Polish historians, but these are extremely tendentious. Furthermore, there is no monograph in any language that covers the topic in its entirety.

Grants from the Center for Slavic and East European Studies at the University of California at Berkeley and a Faculty Research Grant from the University of Tennessee made possible the completion of this project. Some of my findings have appeared, in different contexts, in articles published in the third and fourth volumes of *California Slavic Studies* and the fifteenth volume of *The Polish Review*.

C ONTENTS

THE POLISH QUESTION

IN THE RUSSIAN STATE DUMA

I

INTRODUCTION: RUSSO-POLISH RELATIONS

IN THE NINETEENTH CENTURY

IN THE LONG AND TEMPESTUOUS HISTORY of Russo-Polish relations, dramatic confrontations and hostile exchanges have seldom been lacking. Not even partition and loss of political independence sufficed to still Polish national aspirations and Russian fears of them. In the century between the Congress of Vienna in 1815 and the resurrection of a Polish state in 1918, the theme of Polish freedom and independence from hated Russian rule indelibly stamped the mutual attitudes of Russians and Poles. However, following the Polish uprising of 1863, this theme was considerably muted. With the collapse of the January insurrection and the failure of the liberal Western powers to intervene effectively, the hope for independence from autocratic Russia, which the Poles had nourished for half a century, now disappeared almost completely. In general, the first half of the century of Polish subjection to Russia was characterized by romantically inspired armed conflict, enthusiastically endorsed by liberal European opinion. The second half of the century was marked by the undramatic, positivistic, daily struggle to preserve the national identity and language against Russification, a period during which the Polish question was

3

viewed with increasing indifference by most Europeans. The Congress of Vienna inaugurated what appeared to be a promising phase in Russo-Polish relations. Emperor Alexander I of Russia approached the Polish question under the influence of his old friend and confidant, Prince Adam Czartoryski. Czartoryski belonged to one of the leading aristocratic families of Poland and had been both a member of Alexander's unofficial committee and, for a time, his foreign minister. Under his influence, and despite Polish support of Napoleon, Alexander insisted on undoing the crime of the partitions of Poland and reconstituting the Polish Kingdom with himself as constitutional king. Although Alexander was obliged to leave Great Poland and Galicia with Prussia and Austria, the bulk of Napoleon's Grand Duchy of Warsaw went to Russia and was constituted as the Kingdom of Poland, or the Congress Kingdom. A constitution was prepared, largely by Czartoryski.

On paper, the constitution of 1815 was one of the most liberal in Europe at the time. The franchise was granted to about one hundred thousand citizens, a larger number than in Restoration France. Poland received its own political institutions and army, separate from those of Russia. Polish was the official language. The constitution guaranteed freedom of person and press and the inviolability of property. There was a bicameral legislature, the upper house being composed of the church hierarchy and the aristocracy and the lower house of the gentry and the prosperous urban class. The legislature had the right to examine but not to initiate legislation. The emperor of Russia, as king of Poland, retained full executive power, the right of legislative initiative, and an absolute veto. The main consultive body was the Council of State nominated by the king.

Czartoryski was a member of the Council of State, but

the highest office of viceroy was entrusted to the more obedient and unambitious General Józef Zajączek. The viceroy acted through the executive agency of an Administrative Council. After Zajączek's death in 1826, the office of viceroy was not filled and the Administrative Council exercised its powers. In addition, Nicholas Novosiltsev, a liberal turned reactionary, became the influential imperial commissioner to the Polish government. A Secretariat of State of the Kingdom of Poland was established in St. Petersburg. Also, the Polish army was commanded by Alexander I's brother, the autocratic and brutal Grand Duke Constantine, who, in practice, was more important than the government. Furthermore, the Lithuanian, Belorussian, and Ukrainian territories of the old Polish Commonwealth remained integral parts of Russia and permanent objectives in the expectancies of Polish nationalists, who desired a total reconstruction of pre-partition Poland.

Nevertheless, the fact that Grand Duke Constantine's military command was spread to five western Russian provinces encouraged Polish hopes that these borderlands would be reunited with the Kingdom. Alexander himself maintained these hopes when, in 1818, he opened the first session of the Polish parliament, the Sejm, in Warsaw and declared that he might be able "to extend what I have done for you." In addition, despite the political loss of the borderlands by the Poles, Polish cultural influence in the area actually increased in the early nineteenth century. Czartoryski was particularly active in this respect and devoted his main energies to the Vilno Educational District of which he was the curator and which embraced Lithuania, Belorussia, and the Ukraine. In 1802, he opened a Polish university in Vilno which became the main Polish academic center. A network of secondary and primary schools was also founded in the educational district, and an exceptionally high academic level was maintained in particular by the lyceum of Krzemieniec in Volhynia.

However, Alexander's increasingly reactionary policies and the dissatisfaction of Polish nationalists with the political union of Poland and Russia darkened the prospects of a lasting Russo-Polish reconciliation. Despite the specific provisions of the Polish constitution, censorship was introduced in 1819; secret police activities and political arrests began. Czartoryski was removed from his curatorship in 1824.

During the second session of the Sejm in 1820, many protests against the government's violation of the constitution were voiced, and a majority of the government's bills were rejected. The next Sejm was not summoned until 1825, and the emperor arbitrarily decreed that its deliberations not be public and that the leaders of the opposition be excluded from it. It was at this time that secret societies of radical Polish patriots began to be formed in the 1820's among students and army officers. In 1821 the Patriotic Society was organized, with branches not only in the Kingdom, but also in Poznań, Lithuania, and Volhynia, as well as in the army. Members of the society established contacts with the Russian Decembrists, army conspirators who were planning to overthrow the autocracy.

The sudden death of Alexander I in 1825 precipitated a crisis in Russian policy toward Poland. The new tsar, Nicholas I, disliked the constitutional system granted to the Congress Kingdom by his more idealistic eldest brother, and there was no more talk of a territorial or substantive extension of Polish autonomy. The connections between the Decembrists and the Patriotic Society were disclosed and the latter was suppressed. The mild treatment of the society's members by a special Polish court was at first the source of some conflict, but Nicholas, who desired Polish support in his Turkish war of 1828–1829 and in a possible war with Austria, did not press the matter. His coming to Warsaw to be crowned king of Poland in 1829 was a gesture of reconciliation.

Although there was no question of brutal Russian oppression, mutual distrust now prevailed, and the cordiality in Russo-Polish relations that had accompanied the creation of the Congress Kingdom and had been later undermined by Alexander I was finally destroyed by Nicholas I. A new conspiratorial society was formed in 1828 among cadets of the officers' training school in Warsaw, who detested Grand Duke Constantine's arbitrary and stringent discipline of the army. The outbreak in July 1830 of the revolution in France, which overthrew the Bourbon dynasty, and the success of the Belgian revolution in August inflamed romantic Polish patriots. Their feelings were intensified by their fear that Nicholas was prepared to use the Polish army in the event that he should undertake military intervention against French revolutionaries. A climax was reached on the evening of November 29, 1830, when conspirators seized the official residence of Grand Duke Constantine. Later that night, the arsenal was broken into and arms were distributed.

Nicholas issued a manifesto condemning the uprising and demanding that the Poles return to their allegiance to him. However, the Sejm deposed Nicholas, demanded the reunion of the eastern territories of the old Commonwealth with the Kingdom, and formed a national government under Czartoryski. War with Russia was now inevitable and the results could hardly be in doubt. Warsaw was occupied by Russian forces in September 1831, and effective Polish resistance came to an end. Uprisings in Lithuania and the Ukraine were also put down. Despite the fact that the uprising aroused romantic and liberal sympathy in Europe, there was never any question of armed intervention by any power. Furthermore, intellectual Russians were mostly hostile to Polish aspirations: not only to the demand for the return of Russia's western provinces but also to the desire for the reestablishment of an independent Poland. Even Pushkin in his poetry protested against foreign sympathy for the faithless Poles.

After the November uprising, many Polish political leaders, including Czartoryski, emigrated to western Europe, and the Congress Kingdom began to suffer the burden of defeat and reprisal. The Polish army was disbanded. A Russian army of occupation was commanded by the victor of the war of 1830, Field Marshal I. F. Paskevich, who also became viceroy of Poland. About 10 percent of the large landed estates belonging to participants in the insurrection were confiscated. The constitution of 1815 was abrogated and replaced by the Organic Statute of 1832, which guaranteed the separate administration of Poland but strongly limited it. The Sejm disappeared and the effective control of affairs was placed in the hands of the viceroy, who became the autocratic ruler of the Kingdom, which was kept in a state of emergency. The highest posts in the government were held by Russians. The middle and lower ranks of the administration were staffed by Poles, but the provincial authorities were placed under Russian military commanders. A citadel was erected in Warsaw to intimidate the capital. The universities of Vilno and Warsaw and the lyceum of Krzemieniec were closed down. In 1837, the Polish voivodships (*województwa*) were renamed Russian provinces (*gubernii*) and, in 1844, their number was reduced to five. The Russian monetary system was introduced in 1841. The Russian criminal code was also promulgated, although the Napoleonic Civil Code was maintained in

8

effect. All educational matters were placed directly under the Ministry of Education in St. Petersburg.

MAP 1. THE CONGRESS KINGDOM OF POLAND AND RUSSIA'S
NINE WESTERN PROVINCES

In Russia's western provinces, the policy of oppression was much more severe than in the Kingdom, where the Polish language at least remained official for administrative and educational purposes. In Lithuania and the Ukraine, a campaign was undertaken to wipe out Polish influence. Many minor gentry lost their nobility, had their property confiscated, or were deported to other parts of the Empire. Official policy was particularly harsh toward the Uniate

Church. The Polish government had made the attempt by the Synods of Brest in 1595–1596 to subordinate the Orthodox Church in the Commonwealth to the papacy while allowing it to retain its liturgy, rites, and hierarchy. The consequence was a split between the Uniates and the Orthodox. After the partitions of Poland, the Uniate Church had enjoyed broad tolerance under Alexander I. However, in 1839, the Church was abolished in Russia's western provinces, and several million Belorussians and Ukrainians were forcibly converted to the official Russian Orthodox faith. The Uniate Church was preserved in the Kingdom only in the diocese of Chełm.

One international consequence of the suppression of the insurrection of 1830 was the renewed collaboration among the three partitioning powers of Poland—Russia, Austria, and Prussia. The agreements of Münchengrätz in 1833 provided for cooperation among the three powers in combating Polish conspiracies and for the reciprocal extradition of political refugees.

Exiled Poles engaged actively in the revolutions of 1848, especially in the Hungarian national uprising directed against Austria. When Nicholas I sent Paskevich to help the Austrians, the emperor declared in his manifesto that he would fight not only the Hungarian but also the Polish rebels. Little came of negotiations conducted before and during the Crimean War between England, France, and Turkey and the exiled Czartoryski for the formation of a Polish legion and the recognition of Poland as a belligerent power. During the peace negotiations in the winter of 1855–1856, the possibility was raised in England and France of obliging Russia to reconstitute the Congress Kingdom of 1815, but nothing was accomplished.

However, Russia's defeat in the Crimean War and the deaths of Nicholas I in 1855 and Paskevich in 1856 inaugurated a change in Russia's Polish policy. At the peace congress in Paris, the head of the Russian delegation, Prince Alexis F. Orlov, assured Emperor Napoleon III that the new ruler of Russia, Alexander II, would modify Russia's attitude toward the Poles. The inexorable Paskevich was succeeded as viceroy by the gentler Prince Michael D. Gorchakov. Many Polish prisoners in Siberia and émigrés were amnestied and allowed to return to Poland. On a visit to Warsaw in 1856, Alexander warned the Polish nobility against political "reveries," but the state of emergency was lifted that year and a series of moderate concessions was made. Russian censorship was eased somewhat. The University of Warsaw was not reopened but, in 1857, a medical academy was founded. An agricultural society was also established. Guided by Count Andrzej Zamoyski, a nephew of Adam Czartoryski, it provided the landowners with a forum to discuss broad social and political issues. Zamoyski, the leader of "organic work," believed in a policy of collaboration with Russia as a means of obtaining reforms and a temporary renunciation of nationalist ambitions.

The most important Polish spokesman for the policy of Russo-Polish cooperation was Marquis Aleksander Wielopolski, who attempted to revive Czartoryski's initial program. Wielopolski's policy was to abandon the struggle for national independence and accept the inevitable fact of Russian rule which, however, he hoped to make more acceptable by the creation of new Polish political institutions and the implementation of various reforms. Wielopolski's policy was sharply opposed by Polish radicals, many of whom were recruited from groups of intellectuals, students, and young army officers. The radicals believed that by pursuing an activist course toward permanent revolution they could prevent a reconciliation between the moderates and the Russian government and thereby wrest Polish independence from Russia. They were inspired by Garibaldi and the unification of Italy. Wielopolski also lacked the support of the moderates like Zamoyski, who feared that their patriotism would be questioned if they collaborated with the authorities.

Two radically inspired mass demonstrations in February 1861 caused the emperor to appoint Wielopolski the head of a new Commission of Religion and Education, but Zamoyski declined to cooperate with Viceroy Gorchakov. Further demonstrations led to the proclamation of martial law by St. Petersburg. After months of hesitation, Alexander II agreed to grant certain concessions in order to pacify the country. In 1862, Wielopolski was appointed chief of the civil administration in Poland and the emperor's brother, the liberal Grand Duke Constantine, was appointed viceroy. Also, Poles were named governors in all five Polish provinces. The reforms promulgated by Wielopolski included: the conversion of the economic obligations of peasants to landowners from labor services to money rents, the creation of a State Council as the highest authority under the viceroy, and the inauguration of a system of local self-government through elected urban and district councils. In addition, Jews were granted equal rights, and a law on public education expanded the system of schools. The University of Warsaw, suppressed after 1831, was reopened under the name of Main School. However, these concessions did not win Wielopolski popular support. Zamoyski's followers demanded the extension of reforms to Lithuania and the Ukraine as parts of Poland. These demands were unacceptable to the Russians and Zamoyski was banished abroad. The radicals refused to accept concessions from Russia and give up their plans for an insurrection. Wielopolski finally decided to prevent such a possibility by conscripting 10,000 young men into the army.

The conscription measures precipitated the denouement in January 1863 when the rebellion broke out. The uprising of 1863 differed essentially from that of 1830 in that the Poles had no regular army and held none of the large cities. The result was a guerilla war that lasted until 1864, when the last leader of the uprising, Romuald Traugutt, was executed. Moreover, as in 1831, widespread sympathy in France and England for the Polish cause did not carry over from diplomatic protests to military intervention. Furthermore, Bismarck concluded with Russia the Alvensleben Convention, which provided for cooperation between the Russian and Prussian forces in the frontier area against Polish insurgents and allowed the Russians to pursue Polish fugitives into Prussia.

In the half-century following the failure of the 1863 uprising, the Polish question lost its significance to the rest of Europe, and, for the first forty years, Russian Poland was subjected to a policy of stubborn and unrelenting repression and Russification. One significant reform, the final emancipation of the peasants, was introduced, but it produced consequences quite different from those intended by its sponsors. This emancipation in 1864 followed the emancipation of the Russian serfs in 1861. The settlement in Poland was more advantageous to the peasants and less favorable to the landowners than had been the case in Russia proper, but the aim of the government in Poland was to weaken the gentry and to win the peasants away from the rebellious upper class and make them loyal and satisfied Russian subjects. The law of 1864 granted the peasants the ownership of the land they worked and maintained their rights to the use of woods and pastures. In contrast to the peasants of Russia, the Polish peasants were not required to pay redemption dues for the acquisition of the land. The previous owners received their compensation in bonds and on much less favorable terms than the Russian landowners had received in 1861. The land reform laws also provided for a new structure of local administration. Unlike the Russian *volost'* system whereby the peasants were legally separated from other social classes, the Polish commune (*gmina*) included gentry landowners as well as peasants and was strictly supervised by government officials. However, the land reform did not achieve its official aim of reconciling the mass of the Polish nation to Russian rule. In fact, it had quite the opposite effect. It helped to create a strong middle class among the peasantry and to break down traditionally rigid class barriers. In the fifty years after 1864, patriotic values that had at one time been largely confined to the gentry were more widely diffused among other social levels; Russian officialdom came to be looked upon as the main enemy by most classes of Polish society.

On the basis of the emancipation laws, the Russian government believed that it could completely unify the Kingdom with the Empire, suppressing any separate Polish political existence and replacing local Polish administrators with Russians. Grand Duke Constantine continued to advocate a policy of mildness and restraint, but the emperor disagreed, and Constantine was replaced as viceroy by General Theodore Berg, who pursued a policy of severity, particularly after an unsuccessful attempt on his life in 1863. The Kingdom's separate institutions were almost completely abolished during the decade of Berg's rule. The Secretariat of State of the Kingdom of Poland in St. Petersburg, the Council of State, the Administrative Council, and the various government commissions disappeared. Henceforth, all matters handled by these agencies were dealt with by the central government of the Empire and the administrative distinction of the Kingdom from the Empire was eliminated. In 1867, the former Kingdom was divided into ten smaller provinces, each having a Russian governor. When Berg died in 1874, the office of viceroy was abolished and replaced by that of a governor general, who was in command of the Warsaw Military District and who held in his hands supreme military, civil, and police authority. The name "Kingdom of Poland" was replaced in official usage by "the Vistula region" (*privislinskii krai*) or "Vistula provinces" (*privislinskie gubernie*). In 1876, the Russian judicial system, with the exception of the institution of the jury, was introduced, and the Warsaw Judicial District was subordinated to the Ministry of Justice. The Napoleonic Civil Code, however, remained in force. Various states of emergency remained in effect almost without interruption until 1914. The press was subject in effect to preventive censorship. The institutions of urban and rural self-government which existed in Russia were not extended to Poland; communal government was controlled by district officials. The new administrative apparatus was staffed almost exclusively by Russian officials and Russian was the only authorized official language.

The greatest efforts of the government were expended on the Russification of education. The Main School in Warsaw was replaced in 1869 by a Russian University of Warsaw with Russian as the language of instruction. Whereas the Main School had had almost 1,300 students enrolled when it was closed, the University of Warsaw had only 445 in 1876. In 1866–1869, Russian was introduced as the language of instruction in the secondary schools. Polish remained an optional subject and the language had to be taught in Russian; only religion might be taught in Polish. In 1885, Russian was introduced as the language of instruction in primary schools, and only the Polish language and the Catholic religion were to be taught in Polish. The struggle with the Polish language reached its greatest intensity under Governor General I. V. Gurko (1883–1894) and A. L. Apukhtin, the curator of the Warsaw Educational District (1879–1897). During this period of "the Apukhtin night," the number of schools decreased, illiteracy increased, and the level of education in Poland began to fall beneath that of Russia.

In order to make the Catholic Church in Poland its obedient instrument, the Russian government decided to subordinate the hierarchy and sever its connections with Rome. In 1864, all church property was confiscated and most monasteries were closed. The entire clergy was to be paid by the state. The government broke the Concordat of 1847 with Rome and, in 1867, the whole church hierarchy was placed under the authority of the Spiritual College in St. Petersburg. Pope Pius IX did not recognize this institution and forbade the bishops to send representatives to it. There followed a series of conflicts between the episcopate and the government. Recalcitrant bishops were exiled, and in 1870 not a single bishop in the Kingdom remained in his diocese. It was only after the election of Leo XIII as pope that relations between Russia and the Vatican were normalized. In 1882, a *modus vivendi* was reached and the vacant episcopal sees were filled. On the other hand, the Russian government decided to liquidate completely the Uniate Church in the only remaining diocese, that of Chełm. In 1875, the Uniate Church was abolished in Poland and the population was converted to Orthodoxy. A new Orthodox bishopric was created in Chełm. Those faithful who resisted conversion were fiercely and brutally punished with flogging and exile, and no conversions to Latin Catholicism were allowed. Efforts were made to further the cause of Orthodoxy wherever possible. An Orthodox eparchy of Poland had been established in 1840, and an

Orthodox cathedral was now erected in the center of Warsaw. Rightly considered a symbol of Russification, it was razed in 1919.

The insurrection of 1863 was put down with particular severity in Lithuania, where an attempt was made to eradicate the Polish element entirely. Lithuania, unlike the Congress Kingdom, had been considered from the time of the partitions of Poland an integral part of the Empire. In May 1863, Michael N. Muraviev was appointed governor general of Lithuania, or "the northwestern region" (*severozapadnyi krai*), as the three provinces of Vilno, Grodno, and Kovno were henceforth officially denominated. Called "the hangman," Muraviev pursued a policy of terror toward the insurgents of 1863 that was more brutal and more massive than Viceroy Berg's policy in Poland. Also, after the repression of the uprising, systematic anti-Polish measures were maintained. Poles might inherit but not purchase land. In addition to the confiscation by the Russian government of land from insurgents, politically suspect persons were obliged to sell their estates. Moreover, all Polish landowners had to pay a special annual tax of 10, and then 5, percent of their income. This tribute remained in effect to the beginning of the twentieth century. The Lithuanian provinces did not receive the institutions of local self-government that had been introduced in Russia. Russification of the administration, courts, and school system was complete. The Polish language was eliminated from commercial correspondence and shop signs, and the Catholic clergy were even prohibited from keeping civil registry books in Polish. As a result of official policies in Lithuania, the percentage of the gentry considering itself Polish declined appreciably, but the social and economic position of the Polish upper class in the officially named "southwestern region" (*iugozapadnyi krai*), the provinces of Kiev,

Volhynia, and Podolia, remained relatively unaffected after 1863. The area was outside of Muraviev's control and the uprising in the region had not assumed extensive proportions.

The accession to the Russian throne in 1894 of a new emperor, Nicholas II, appeared at first to augur a relaxation in the pressure of Russification. Relations with the Vatican improved; in a papal brief to the Polish bishops, Pope Leo XIII urged clerical and lay obedience to the Russian state, and Russia appointed a resident minister to the Vatican. Gurko and Apukhtin were removed from office. The succeeding governors general, Count P. A. Shuvalov and Prince A. K. Imeretinskii, established friendly relations with the Polish aristocracy. In 1897, the young emperor visited Warsaw and was welcomed with a declaration of loyalty by a committee under Zygmunt Wielopolski, the son of Aleksander and the representative of a policy of Russo-Polish reconciliation. A gift to the emperor of a million rubles was assigned to the construction of a Polytechnic Institute, with Russian as the language of instruction. Permission was also granted for the erection in Warsaw of a statue of Adam Mickiewicz, the Polish national poet. However, nothing came of these gestures and the official attitude toward the Polish question underwent no change. Furthermore, Polish Socialists succeeded in obtaining, and publishing in London in 1898, a secret memorandum of Prince Imeretinskii in which it was disclosed that no official concessions to the Poles were being contemplated.

It was the revolution of 1905 and the establishment in Russia of a quasi-constitutional political system that first revealed the possibility of a genuine change for the better in Russo-Polish relations. And despite the heavy burden of Russification and political oppression, many Polish spokesmen were prepared to cooperate with reformist elements in the Empire's transformed regime to help bring about the change. Various factors contributed to this cooperative attitude. Despite the brutal repression after 1863, the Congress Kingdom entered an era of rapid industrialization and modernization that benefited most classes, including many of the impoverished gentry class who entered the intellectual and professional classes in the cities. The disasters of 1830 and 1863 had taught the folly of direct military confrontation with Russia. The new formulas were "organic work" and "triple loyalty" to the three partitioning powers. The Poles were adjured to create a modern society, to renounce romantic dreams of national independence, and to exploit the vast economic opportunities presented by the inclusion of Poland within the Russian Empire. Late in the nineteenth century, more activist programs developed. The Socialist movement acquired significance at the end of the 1880's but was divided between those who desired to perpetuate the radical, nationalist, and insurrectionary tradition of the nineteenth century and those who rejected Polish nationalism and believed in the strictly international Social Democratic movement.

Non-Socialist radicalism also revived during the 1880's and was influenced by Bismarck's strongly anti-Polish policy in Prussia in the late 1870's. It rejected the formula of triple loyalty in favor of preparations for a new uprising that, this time, would embrace all parts of pre-partition Poland and would involve the nationally awakened broad masses of the population on the basis of political, social, and economic justice. Its first organization, the Polish League, was founded in Switzerland in 1887. It organized patriotic demonstrations and created a secret school organization to foster Polish national consciousness. Among its leaders was Roman Dmowski, the principal nationalist ideologist of the early twentieth century. In 1893, Dmowski transformed the Polish League into a National League and moved its secret headquarters to Warsaw. *Przegląd Wszechpolski*, the theoretical journal of the league, was first published in Galicia in 1895.

Dmowski was influenced by Darwinian concepts of biological nationalism, sacred national egoism, and political realism. He came to oppose as chimerical the ideology of insurrection although, until 1905, he also opposed meek collaboration by the Poles with the oppressive tsarist regime. Dmowski believed that Germany constituted the main danger to Poland's national existence. Russia, on the other hand, with its vast industrial and commercial potentialities, presented great opportunities to skilled and educated Poles. However, the Russian government would have to retreat from its policy of repression and grant its Polish subjects civil and political liberties, a degree of self-government, and reasonable national self-determination, including the official use of the Polish language. Only then might Russia count on Polish support in the eventuality of a war with Germany. In 1897, the National League was replaced by the National Democratic party, the principal rival of the Socialists for political leadership in the Congress Kingdom. In line with Dmowski's views, the party program of 1903 renounced the possibility of armed or diplomatic activity directed toward national independence in favor of a firm but legal defense of the Polish cause—a revival of the formulas of organic work and triple loyalty. The National Democratic party soon became the spokesman for wide sections of the urban middle class, intellectuals, and well-to-do peasants in Poland.

During the Russo-Japanese War, the National Democrats adopted a waiting attitude. Dmowski traveled to Tokyo in 1904 and urged the Japanese not to consider plans to encourage an insurrection in Poland against Russia because it could not possibly succeed and would do the Poles more harm than good. The policy of the National Democrats during the first half of 1905 when the Congress Kingdom was swept by industrial and school strikes was to avoid violence but to press for the grant by the Russian government of Polish autonomy within the Empire.

The entire political situation affecting Russians as well as Poles appeared to be transformed by the success of the revolution of 1905 culminating in the general strike in the second half of October that brought public life in Russia to a standstill. Faced by the choice of either making concessions to the immense opposition movement to the autocracy that had been discredited by humiliating defeat at the hands of the Japanese or else attempting to establish a military dictatorship, Nicholas II and his government finally capitulated. The Emperor issued the October Manifesto that converted the Romanov autocracy into a constitutional monarchy.

The October Manifesto of 1905 promising Russia a constitution, general elections, and a genuine legislative assembly, as well as guaranteeing civil liberties, seemed to open a new era of freedom and to hold out the prospect of a substantial betterment in the position of Russia's Poles. The existence of a Russian parliament signified that views and policies different from the unyielding official line in Poland might be advocated and implemented. The years of relative calm between revolution and war, from 1905 to 1914, offered the one opportunity of the time for a meaningful and reasonable Russo-Polish dialogue in the forum of the State Duma. The constitutional experiment caused Poles to look to St. Petersburg with fresh hope.

II

THE REVOLUTION OF 1905

AND THE POLISH QUESTION

AFTER 1905, the ancient conflict between the Russian autocracy and its Polish subjects assumed new dimensions
with the establishment of a Russian parliament and political parties and with political reorientations in Poland itself.
To be sure, the approach of the government hardly altered.
Despite the worsening of Russia's relations with Germany
and Austria-Hungary at the beginning of the century, no
radical departures occurred in the official policy of Russification. The Poles continued to be regarded with suspicion; any concessions to them were made grudgingly and
under duress, while the principal Polish political demand,
that of some form of autonomy, was firmly rejected.

However, in conforming with the imperial decree of December 12, 1904, "on the improvement of the system of
government" with its promise of reforms in the system of
local self-government as well as a review of existing limitations on the rights of the national minorities, the Committee
of Ministers discussed the Polish question from March to
May of 1905. Its conclusions were accepted by the emperor
in June. It was decided to make certain concessions on the
use of Polish in schools and rural administration and to re-

move in principle the existing restrictions on Poles from entering government service. On the other hand, with regard to the issue of introducing into the Kingdom institutions of self-government, nothing was resolved except to instruct the governor general, G. A. Skalon, to elaborate preliminary proposals for urban self-government. The possibility of introducing rural self-government modeled on the modest and limited Russian zemstvo system was not admitted, much less that of any broadly defined political autonomy.[1]

The ameliorative measures actually decreed by the government were meager. The decree of April 17, 1905, on religious tolerance was applied to Poland and was followed by mass reconversions to Roman Catholicism among the mixed Polish-Ukrainian population of eastern Siedlce and Lublin, which had been forcibly converted from the Uniate Church to Greek Orthodoxy after 1875.[2] The decree of May 1, 1905, removed restrictions on the acquisition of property by Poles in the nine western provinces of Russia. It also permitted the teaching of Polish and Lithuanian in the schools in districts where a majority of the students were Polish or Lithuanian.[3] The statute of June 6, 1905, and the decree of October 1, 1905, allowed the functioning of private secondary schools in Poland with Polish as the primary language of instruction, although the Russian language, history, and geography had to be taught in Russian.

[1] Zygmunt Łukawski, "Rosyjskie ugrupowania polityczne wobec sprawy autonomii Królestwa Polskiego w okresie 1905–1917 (W świetle archiwalnych materiałów rosyjskich)," *Zeszyty naukowe Uniwersytetu Jagiellońskiego. Prace historyczne*, 9 (1962), 149–51. Beginning with this chapter, dates are given Old Style.

[2] Henryk Wiercieński, *Ziemia Chełmska i Podlasie. Rys historyczny i obraz stanu dzisiejszego* (Warsaw, 1919), p. 25.

[3] N. I. Lazarevskii, *Zakonodatel'nye akty perekhodnago vremeni 1904–1908 gg.*, 3rd ed. (St. Petersburg, 1909), pp. 52–54. The provinces were those of Vilno, Kovno, Grodno, Minsk, Mogilev, Vitebsk, Kiev, Podolia, and Volhynia.

In state secondary schools, Catholic religious instruction and the Polish language might be taught in Polish. In the elementary schools, only religion, arithmetic, and the Polish language were allowed to be taught in Polish. A private organization, Mother of Polish Schools (*Polska Macierz Szkolna*), founded about eight hundred elementary schools in the Kingdom. However, this organization was closed in December 1907 on the instructions of the governor general. The limited use of Polish, along with Russian, in communal government and in the internal transactions of private societies was also permitted.[4] In 1906, a chair of Polish literature, with instruction to be given in Polish, was established at the University of Warsaw.[5]

However, in December 1905, when Count Ivan I. Tolstoi, the minister of education, proposed further extensions in the use of Polish in public schools as "the principal condition for calming minds and establishing normal life in the country," he was strongly opposed by Governor General Skalon: "The fact must not be lost sight of that should the desires of Polish nationalists in the school issue be fully satisfied, the government itself will be the first to put its hand to the realization of the systematic plan of the Poles to establish the autonomy of Poland." Tolstoi's proposal was not even discussed by the Council of Ministers.[6] Furthermore, only ten days after the promulgation of the October Manifesto, martial law was proclaimed throughout the ten provinces of the Kingdom on the grounds that Polish political leaders desired the independence of Poland from Russia. This charge was later modified to one that "all classes of the Polish population and all political parties

---

[4] *Ibid.*, pp. 63–67, 143–44.

[5] Józef Siemieński, ed., *La Pologne. Son histoire, son organisation et sa vie* (Lausanne-Paris, 1918), p. 454.

[6] P. Gorin, "Natsional'naia politika tsarizma v Pol'she v XX veke," *Bor'ba klassov*, 10 (1933), 65.

have been seized by the thought of Polish autonomy." At the beginning of December, martial law was lifted by an imperial decree and the complete pacification of Poland was proclaimed. However, three weeks later, Skalon on his own initiative reintroduced martial law in all ten provinces; this state of affairs was maintained until October 1908.[7]

At the end of 1905, the non-Socialist Polish political parties organized a delegation under the conciliatory National Democratic leader Roman Dmowski to see Prime Minister Sergius Iu. Witte and to request the Polonization of the state schools as well as a constituent assembly, the latter demand opposed by Dmowski himself as "completely unreal."[8] On the way to St. Petersburg, the delegation learned of the declaration of martial law in Poland, and a majority of the delegates returned to Warsaw without having seen Witte. Dmowski was invited informally to an interview with the prime minister and assured him that the separation of Poland from Russia was "an unattainable dream."[9] When asked by Witte what had to be done in order to pacify Poland, Dmowski replied that civil authority must be placed in the hands of the Poles. Witte countered that this was impossible since military authority in the area had to remain under Russian control and, if the Poles were given civil authority, a conflict would immediately follow between the two nationalities. Dmowski answered by sharply criticizing official policy in Poland as leading inevitably to a catastrophe.[10]

Nevertheless, despite the Russian government's unyielding position, there were two new factors in Russo-Polish

[7] Leon Wasilewski, *Rosja wobec Polaków w dobie "konstitucyjnej"* (Kraków, 1916), p. 12; also Siemieński, *La Pologne*, p. 421.
[8] Roman Dmowski, *Polityka polska i odbudowanie państwa*, 2nd ed. (Warsaw, 1926), p. 56.
[9] S. Iu. Witte, *Vospominaniia* (Moscow, 1960), III, 164.
[10] Dmowski, *Polityka polska*, pp. 56–58.

relations after 1905. In the first place, by the early twentieth century the majority of the influential Polish political leaders in the Congress Kingdom were pursuing a generally conciliatory policy toward the government. They were abandoning the traditional nineteenth-century demand for independence combined with a military uprising against Russia in favor of the demand for Polish political autonomy along the lines of the constitution of 1815 within the framework of what they hoped was to become a liberalized Russia.[11] The most prominent advocate of this more narrowly defined nationalism of self-interest was Dmowski. The second factor was the emergence of new Russian political groupings. Except for those groups of the right wing, they adopted more or less favorable positions with regard to various Polish grievances. However, it should be recognized that the creation of a Russian parliament had the necessary consequence of transferring vague sentiments concerning policy into the arena of political actions with often unexpected consequences when Russian liberalism and nationalism came into conflict. As for the extremes of the political spectrum, the rightist parties adhered to an ultra-Russian nationalism. Their programs made no mention of autonomy for the Congress Kingdom, nor did they advocate any relaxation in official policies in Poland.[12] At the other end of the political spectrum, the Social Democratic and Socialist Revolutionary programs defended the right of the nationalities to political self-determination.[13]

In liberal Russian political circles, discussion of the

[11] Marian Kukiel, *Dzieje Polski porozbiorowe* (London, 1961), p. 470; Władysław Pobóg-Malinowski, *Najnowsza historia polityczna Polski*, 2nd ed. (London, 1963), I, 507; Wilhelm Feldman, *Dzieje polskiej myśli politycznej 1864–1914*, 2nd ed. (Warsaw, 1933), p. 276.

[12] V. Ivanovich, *Rossiiskie partii, soiuzy i ligi. Sbornik ustavov, programm i spravochnykh svedenii* (St. Petersburg, 1906), p. 119 (Union of the Russian People), p. 129 (Russian Assembly).

[13] *Ibid.*, pp. 5, 11.

Polish question began in 1904, particularly in the St. Petersburg daily newspaper *Rus'* and in Peter B. Struve's émigré *Osvobozhdenie*. The latter advocated a transformation of Russo-Polish relations on the basis of the constitution granted to Poland in 1815 by Alexander I. The constitution should be the model used in formulating new policy.[14] The first direct confrontation between Poles and Russian liberals took place in Paris in November 1904. Among the Poles were Dmowski and Józef Piłsudski, the leader of the Polish Socialist party. Struve, Paul N. Miliukov, and Prince Paul D. Dolgorukov represented Russian liberalism. Both sides agreed on cooperation against the regime and on freedom of development for the nationalities. Specifically, the Poles recognized the unity and sovereignty of the Russian state in return for a promise of Polish autonomy. However, the meeting also demonstrated differences of opinion among the Russians regarding the Polish question, and no formula for Polish autonomy was agreed upon. Miliukov in particular was quite reserved. The Polish question was "controversial" and the debates ended with "an extremely reserved" resolution. He opposed the idea of a constituent assembly in Warsaw as "contrary to the concept of autonomy."[15] Miliukov conceded that "Struve and our other delegates went further than I in this question. My firm opposition . . . had the effect that no formula acceptable to both sides was worked out."[16]

Then, in April 1905, the program of the Union of Liberation was published after its third congress. Although the

[14] Wojciech Bułat, "Zjazd polsko-rosyjski w Moskwie 21–22 kwietnia 1905 roku," *Studia z najnowszych dziejów powszechnych* (Warsaw), 2 (1962), 193.

[15] Paul Miliukov, "Aleksander Lednicki jako rzecznik polsko-rosyjskiego porozumienia," *Przegląd współczesny*, 3 (1939), 26–27.

[16] P. N. Miliukov, *Vospominaniia (1859–1917)* (New York, 1955), I, 243.

Finnish question was discussed separately in terms of the demand for the restoration of all autonomous privileges, Poland was simply listed with certain other areas of the Empire as deserving "the broadest possible provincial self-government."[17] Struve wrote on this point in *Osvobozh-denie.* He asserted that Poland should be treated in the same way as Finland because the statement on provincial self-government either gave Poland too little or else would have to be interpreted so broadly as to go too far in making concessions to the national minorities as a whole apart from the Finns and Poles.

The next meeting of Polish and Russian liberals took place in Moscow in April. The purposes of the meeting were an exchange of views, the elimination of prejudices on both sides, and, it was hoped, the elaboration of a common program. The Poles had prepared a resolution that acknowledged the unity of the state but demanded autonomy based on a constitution to be drawn up by a democratically elected constituent assembly in Warsaw.[18] They believed the main task was to convince the Russians of the necessity of autonomy for the Congress Kingdom. However, the Russians considered the Polish desire for a constituent assembly to be excessive. Miliukov warned that Russian liberal-constitutional circles could not "go beyond certain limits in resolving the Polish question" and that only the revolutionary parties might be amenable to radical demands.[19] Even the Polonophile Fedor I. Rodichev, "the knight without reproach fighting incessantly for the rights of oppressed nations,"[20] was cautious. He asserted the necessity of Polish participation in an all-Russian constituent

---

[17] *Osvobozhdenie,* Nos. 69–70, May 20, 1905.
[18] "Zjazd polsko-rosyjski w Moskwie," *Krytyka,* 7 (1905), 31.
[19] *Ibid.,* pp. 40–41.
[20] Wacław Lednicki, *Pamiętniki* (London, 1967), II, 511.

assembly as a prerequisite for any kind of Polish autonomy.[21] In reply, Aleksander Lednicki, the Pole most highly regarded by Russian liberals, took the role of mediator and explained that the Polish requirements were fully compatible with the desire of the Russians to preserve the territorial unity of the state. He also rejected the idea that Poland had to be reconstituted within the boundaries of 1772 and accepted the principle of an ethnic frontier.[22] The meeting produced a preliminary declaration:

> Recognizing the need of the Kingdom of Poland for autonomy with the preservation of state unity and representation in the Russian parliament but with a separate Sejm chosen on the basis of universal, equal, direct, and secret suffrage without distinctions of nationality and religion, the conference considers it necessary to postpone a detailed definition of boundaries and the scope of this autonomy until the time of a comprehensive study of this question.[23]

It was at this time that Alexander I. Guchkov asserted his views on the Polish question. Guchkov represented the more conservative and cautious minority wing of the Russian liberal and constitutionalist movement that later formed the Octobrist party as against the more radical and adventurous left-wing Kadets led by Miliukov. According to Miliukov, after the April conference when the Polish question was being discussed in the salon of V. A. Morozova, Guchkov "expressed himself sharply against Polish autonomy. I answered him no less sharply and warmly. This quarrel produced a sensation in Moscow. It served later as the first indication of the division between the Kadets and the Octobrists. Guchkov referred to the 'or-

---

[21] "Zjazd polsko-rosyjski," p. 35.
[22] *Ibid.*, pp. 37–38.
[23] *Ibid.*, p. 44.

ganicism' of his 'fundamental' convictions to which he opposed my 'bookishness.'"[24] In the same month of April, Guchkov and Miliukov "crossed swords" over the question of Polish autonomy which was raised at the congress of zemstvo delegates that was then meeting in Moscow. Guchkov argued that only the Polish upper classes were interested in political autonomy and regarded it as "the first step towards the complete separation of Poland from Russia." The majority of the Polish nation were allegedly not concerned about any kind of autonomy. Therefore, Guchkov asserted, it was enough to grant the Poles equal rights with other Russian citizens and introduce into Poland organs of local self-government similar to those functioning in Russia proper.[25]

Guchkov and his followers were in a minority when the zemstvo congresses in September and November 1905 passed resolutions on Poland. The first congress recognized

> as essential, after the establishment of a national, democratic, popular assembly with constitutional rights, the immediate separation of the Kingdom of Poland as a distinct autonomous unity with a Sejm elected on the basis of universal, direct, equal, and secret suffrage, subject to the conditions of the preservation of the state unity of the Empire and the ascertainment of the possibility of correcting the boundaries between the Kingdom of Poland and the neighboring provinces on the basis of joint agreement in conformity with national composition and the wishes of the local population.[26]

The boundary corrections were to be made in the eastern districts of the province of Lublin. These districts were

[24] Miliukov, *Vospominaniia*, I, 273–74.
[25] "Iz vospominanii A. I. Guchkova," *Posledniia novosti*, Aug. 9, 1936.
[26] I. P. Belokonskii, *Zemskoe dvizhenie*, 2nd ed. (Moscow, 1914), p. 375.

to be separated from Poland in return for the addition to Poland of areas in the province of Grodno inhabited by a majority of Poles.[27] The extent of the proposed autonomy and the prerogatives of the Sejm were not specified. After much debate, the November congress confirmed the resolution of the September congress but added that "the solution of the Polish question indicated in this resolution not only has nothing in common with the idea of the separation of Poland from Russia but, on the contrary, is necessary for the permanent guarantee of the unity and strength of the Empire."[28] Polish proposals regarding the powers of the Sejm were read at the congress but were not acted upon.

At the September congress, Guchkov and eleven others had strongly protested the resolution in favor of Polish autonomy as an open attempt to dismember Russia.[29] And although the November congress emphasized the unity of the Empire, he and the leadership core of the Octobrists voted a minority resolution offering Poland urban and rural self-government but refusing autonomy. "Russia's only strength is its unity." The question of autonomy was one of "instinct, feeling, faith," and Guchkov's instinct, that of a Great Russian, was against it.[30] The program of the Octobrist party faithfully reflected this attitude. It spoke of the "unitary character" of the state and a broad development of local self-government as well as the right of the nationalists to satisfy "cultural needs" within the limits imposed by the interests of the state. On the other hand, the program rejected "the idea of federalism" with the single exception that Finland should enjoy "a certain autonomous

---

[27] Łukawski, "Rosyjskie ugrupowania polityczne," p. 153.

[28] Boris Veselovskii, *Istoriia zemstva* (St. Petersburg, 1911), III, 645.

[29] F. Dan and N. Cherevanin, "Soiuz 17 oktabria," *Obshchestvennoe dvizhenie v Rossii v nachale XX-go veka* (St. Petersburg, 1914), III, 173.

[30] B. Veselovskii, "Dvizhenie zemlevladel'tsev," *Obshchestvennoe dvizhenie* (St. Petersburg, 1910), II (2), 18.

governmental structure on the condition that a state tie with the Empire be retained."[31] By contrast, Article 25 of the Kadet program recapitulated the resolution of the September zemstvo congress with the stipulation that the Sejm be elected on the same principles as the Russian national assembly and that the Poles participate in the latter assembly on the same basis as the other parts of the Empire.[32]

Thus, by the end of the year 1905, there were emerging strong differences within the Russian liberal movement concerning the extent of the concessions that Russia ought to make to Poland. The State Duma's course of action would show clearly how these differences would frustrate Polish hopes in the Russian legislature.

[31] Ivanovich, *Rossiiskie partii,* pp. 30–31.
[32] *Ibid.,* p. 16.

III

THE POLES IN THE FIRST
AND SECOND DUMAS

SINCE THE SOCIALIST PARTIES in Poland boycotted the elections to the first State Duma, all thirty-four representatives from the Kingdom, out of a total of fifty-five Poles in the Duma, were National Democrats. Eighteen Poles came from Lithuania, Belorussia, and the Ukraine; one each came from St. Petersburg, Kazan, and Kishinev. The Poles from outside the Kingdom had not been elected exclusively by Poles and wished to avoid accusations of separatism with regard to Russia's western provinces. Consequently, they avoided entering into a single parliamentary party with the Poles from the Kingdom, although they maintained close contacts with them. Therefore, the thirty-four National Democratic deputies organized themselves into a separate party called the Koło (Circle) on the principle of strict parliamentary solidarity. Their program referred to the resolution of the November zemstvo congress and called for the introduction of the question of autonomy at the first session of the Duma as well as the passage of a statute of autonomy.[1] However, contrary to the expectations of the

[1] *Stanowisko stronnictwa demokratyczno-narodowego w chwili obecnej* (Warsaw, 1906), p. 15; Zygmunt Łukawski, *Koło polskie w rosyjskiej dumie państwowej w latach 1906–1909* (Wrocław, 1967), pp. 21–22.

33

Poles, the Kadets did nothing to place the matter on the agenda.

Consequently, in the hope of introducing their demand into the reply to the address from the throne, twenty-seven members of the Polish Koło presented a declaration at the third session of the Duma on April 30, 1906. It asserted that the Kingdom of Poland had been created in 1815 by international treaties and that its constitution had guaranteed "a completely autonomous structure." According to the declaration, Nicholas I's Organic Statute of 1832 had not eliminated the concept of autonomy and it had preserved the separate administration of the country. The Koło argued that this autonomy had later been terminated illegally, by the use of various laws and by administrative decisions that could not juridically be applied to the fundamental relationship between Poland and Russia. The fact that the Fundamental Laws of April 23, 1906, did not use the name Kingdom of Poland was an attempt by the government to exclude from the consideration of the State Duma the question of restoring the due rights of Poland. Because the demands of the Poles for the autonomy had "found a friendly response in the Russian liberation movement," satisfaction was being sought from the Russian national assembly.[2]

The declaration of the Polish Koło was strongly attacked by the Kadets as a "serious disservice to the entire Polish nation" and "the worst of all possible tactics."[3] Miliukov argued that the Poles were mistaken in appealing to historic rights and the guarantees of international law. They were incorrect in seeking to find some sort of legal source independent of the Russian government. They were guilty of "political romanticism." They were turning Polish policy

---

[2] *Gosudarstvennaia Duma. Stenograficheskie otchety* (hereafter cited as GDSO). *1906 god. Sessiia I* (St. Petersburg, 1906), I, 50–51.

[3] *Rech'*, May 3, 1906.

back to the idea of a "restoration," and cruel defeat had been encountered there more than once. To call the Polish question an international one was to be an enemy, not a friend, since an international solution involving Germany could only raise difficulties. Furthermore, statements about rights and treaties took the question beyond the limits of autonomy that had heretofore been the basis for discussions between Poles and Russians.[4]

The Duma's reply to the address from the throne was approved almost unanimously on May 5. It was essentially the version prepared by the Kadets. While defending equal rights for the nationalities, the majority of the Duma advanced no demands for autonomy in the borderlands and limited itself to general phrases about satisfying the "urgent demands" of the separate nationalities.[5] One reason for this was the Kadet desire, in the interest of concord, not to alienate the right wing of the Octobrist party as well as certain peasant and labor deputies.[6] In an open exchange of letters published in *Rech'* on May 6, Lednicki, who was a member of the executive committee of the Kadet party, wrote to Miliukov that the reply to the address from the throne might be construed as a Kadet "refusal" to honor its pledge to support Polish autonomy. Miliukov replied that the Duma's statement about the nationalities could not be identical with the program of a single party and that the Kadets had not altered their position on autonomy in principle or in tactics. However, there might admittedly exist differences between them and the Poles "in the justification

[4] P. N. Miliukov, *God bor'by. Publitsisticheskaia khronika 1905–1906* (St. Petersburg, 1907), pp. 387–89.
[5] *GDSO. 1906 god. Sessiia I,* I, 76.
[6] F. Dan, "Obshchaia politika pravitel'stva i izmenenia v gosudarstvennoi organizatsii v period 1905–1907 gg.," *Obshchestvennoe dvizhenie* (St. Petersburg, 1911), IV (2), 14; S. M. Sidel'nikov, *Obrazovanie i deiatel'nost' pervoi gosudarstvennoi Dumy* (Moscow, 1962), p. 215.

and, consequently, in the conception of that autonomy."[7]

Nonetheless, after the First Duma had been dissolved, the Polish Koło declined to sign the Vyborg Manifesto, the appeal made from Finland to the people of Russia by nearly half of the members of the Duma to offer passive resistance to the authorities. The Poles acted on the grounds that, although the Koło certified its "solidarity with the liberation movement," it was not "empowered" to interfere in Russian affairs.[8] In point of fact, there was too little common ground between the Polish delegates and the radically inclined Duma. The social and political programs of both the liberals and the leftists were too extreme for the Poles and did not concretely take into account the special status of Poland within the Empire. The right and the center were weak and also unsympathetic to the prospect of Polish autonomy.

The practical results of the activity of the Koło in the First Duma were slight. An interpellation was made to the Ministry of Public Instruction regarding the statute of June 6 and the decree of October 1, 1905, which permitted a restricted use of Polish in the school system of the Congress Kingdom. It was charged that the school administration was persisting in the old ways of rigid Russification and dismissing instructors who attempted to implement the new laws. As a result of this interpellation, more than two hundred elementary school teachers who had been dismissed were replaced in their positions. In addition, after the dissolution of the First Duma, a decree based on Article 87 of the Fundamental Laws was issued, removing the penalties for secret instruction in Poland and the western provinces.[9]

Of the thirty-four Poles from the Kingdom in the Second

[7] *Rech'*, May 6, 1906.

[8] K. Zalevskii, "Natsional'nye partii v Rossii," *Obshchestvennoe dvizhenie* (St. Petersburg, 1914), III, 237.

[9] *GDSO. 1906 god. Sessiia I*, II, 1025–29; Łukawski, *Koło polskie*, p. 67.

Duma, twenty-seven were National Democrats. Dmowski became the leader of the group and a somewhat different tactic was adopted. The Poles turned away from the Kadets, whose representation had been reduced from about 170 to 98, and sought to obtain the agreement of Peter A. Stolypin's new ministry to the proposal of autonomy for Poland. Given the rough political balance between right and left in the Second Duma, the Polish vote could be a deciding factor. The fate of many government bills would be effectively in the hands of the Poles, and the Koło believed that, in return for its support of the government, the government would approve moderate Polish proposals. At the same time, the Koło drew within its sphere of influence the twelve representatives of the Polish landowners in Lithuania, Belorussia, and the Ukraine, so that in effect it controlled forty-six votes.[10] The price paid was defense of Polish agrarian interests in Russia's western borderlands. Whereas, in the First Duma, the Poles had recognized in principle the necessity of compulsory land expropriations in the provinces of Russia, while the Kadets had excluded Poland from their own agrarian proposals, in the Second Duma, Dmowski felt obliged to include the nine western provinces of Russia within the category of Poland.

Speaking on the question of agrarian reform on March 19, 1907, Dmowski insisted that the matter should be approached in Russia only after the grant of civil liberties, including "broad local self-government." In Poland, however, agrarian matters and all other social reforms lay in the area of separate local legislation and could be settled only by an autonomous Sejm with a defined relationship to the Russian state. Furthermore, the same should apply to areas with a "nationally mixed population," like the nine

[10] Roman Dmowski, *Niemcy, Rosja, i kwestja polska* (Częstochowa, 1938), p. 118.

37

western provinces. The agrarian question could not be settled for these areas by the State Duma. Laws for them ought to be prepared by local agencies and only then introduced in the Duma.[11]

On April 10, the forty-six Polish members of the Duma introduced the proposal for Polish autonomy. It stated that although the Kingdom of Poland constituted an "inalienable" part of the Russian state, it ought to be administered in internal matters by separate institutions on the basis of its own laws. Poland was to have a Sejm, a Polish governor, and a Secretariat of State in the Council of Ministers. However, the last two were to be appointed by the emperor. Furthermore, although Poland was to have its own court system, treasury, and budget, the authority of the Sejm was not to extend to affairs of the imperial family and court, foreign policy, the army and navy, the Orthodox Church, and cases of "sedition against the supreme authority." No changes were to be introduced in the statute of autonomy without the consent of the Sejm. Although the proposal declared that the initial acts of autonomy in 1815 "have kept their validity up to the present," in fact, it actually envisaged a smaller measure of autonomy than had been accorded Poland in 1815. Recognition of Polish autonomy would insure the loyalty of Poland and strengthen the foundations of the Russian state, "which right now ought to be the first concern of the government." The existing bureaucracy in Poland exemplified "all of the negative aspects of the bureaucracy," and the freedom of Russia and Poland was "almost synonymous." The immediate benefit following the grant of autonomy would be "the return of confidence in the government by the Polish nation."[12]

---

[11] *GDSO. 1907 god. Sessiia II* (St. Petersburg, 1907), I, 742–48.
[12] *Gosudarstvennaia Duma. Sbornik materialov. Vtoroi sozyv 1907 god* (St. Petersburg, 1907), No. 83.

Commenting on the Polish proposal, Miliukov noted that it made "significant concessions to the spirit of political realism" by abstaining from direct references to historical rights or from the demand for a constituent Sejm and by admitting the interests of the Russian state. The proposal also listed matters of imperial interest outside of the Sejm's jurisdiction. On the other hand, Miliukov charged, Polish "national demands" were defined so broadly that their realization could "hardly be counted upon seriously." Instead of delimiting the rights of the Sejm, the proposal delimited questions of imperial interest. The matters removed from the competence of the Duma were so extensive as to make the Sejm in fact a constituent assembly. Administrative authorities defined as belonging to the central government were actually subordinated to local authority. In brief, the proposal for autonomy should have been made in the more acceptable form of "provincial autonomy." Miliukov doubted whether a majority of the Duma would support the resolution without extensive revisions. Even if a majority desired to assist the Koło, such an action would not only be an additional load that might drag the Duma to the bottom but would also arouse international complications, meaning an adverse German reaction.[13]

The Octobrists also rejected the Polish proposal for autonomy at their party congress in May. They passed a resolution condemning the proposal as the first step in the dismemberment of Russia and expressing the hope that the Duma would refuse to accept it.[14] Further to the right, *Novoe vremia* observed that the Poles "have forgotten everything and learned nothing," and that as long as Russia stood firm and did not lose its political reason, it would not

[13] *Rech'*, April 12, 1907.
[14] *Ibid.*, May 12, 1907.

"suffer a second Carthage on the banks of the Vistula."[15] In conformity with parliamentary practice, the Polish proposal had been sent by the president of the Duma, S. A. Muromtsev, to Prime Minister Stolypin and the assistant minister of the interior, A. A. Makarov. However, the Duma received no opinion from the Ministry of the Interior during the remaining two months of the legislature's existence. Moreover, in his declaration to the Duma on March 6, Stolypin, while speaking generally about the introduction of self-government into certain areas of the Empire, including Poland, had referred to his government as "conscious of its duty to preserve the historical legacies of Russia . . . a government steadfast and purely Russian." He had also insisted that any self-government would have to be preceded by the separation in a special administrative unit of localities in which were concentrated a purely Russian population with its own special interests—a reference to the separation of the district of Chełm from Poland. Furthermore, the prime minister's declaration had contained no promise of political autonomy for the Congress Kingdom.[16]

The Koło realized that the campaign for autonomy did not have any real chance of success in the Duma. However, the Koło was anxious that the Duma pass some reform legislation affecting Poland and introduced on May 10 the more moderate proposal of a school bill. The bill was submitted independently of the autonomy bill, which allegedly demanded "a longer time for its preparations, legislative passage, and implementation." The school issue in the Kingdom of Poland, however, was a "burning question." The very limited use of Polish in the state elementary and secondary schools conceded in 1905 had brought "almost no

[15] *Novoe vremia*, April 14, 1907.
[16] *GDSO. 1907 god. Sessiia II*, I, 120.

improvement in the sorrowful condition of the schools," and the bill insisted on the need to restore teaching in the native language. It provided for the introduction in the 1907–1908 school year of instruction in Polish in all state elementary and secondary schools as well as the University of Warsaw. Russians, Lithuanians, and Ukrainians would be taught in their own languages. The study of Russian would be compulsory in intermediate schools. All disabilities against non-Russian teachers and foreigners should be removed.[17]

Thus, the Koło agreed to a postponement of the autonomy issue in return for immediate enactment of the school bill. It expected the government to accede since the discussion of the budget was approaching. The passage of two important measures depended on the votes of the Poles: the quota of army recruits and the budget for 1907. The Poles voted for the former and declared their readiness to fulfill their obligations to the state, their political loyalty, and their refusal to look outside the state for support. Speaking on behalf of the Koło in an address that was well received by the center and right, Henryk Konic declared: "We are fighting and shall not cease to fight the present system of government, but we are not fighting either the state or the Russian people." Insisting that the Polish demand for autonomy remained alive, he also stated that "we defend the necessity for Russia of a strong army. We Poles do not wish our fate in this state to depend on any foreign influences."[18]

At this juncture, the difficulties encountered by the Koło in winning the support of a majority of the members of the Duma for Polish proposals were illustrated by the Zurabov incident. In his speech on the quota of recruits, the Social

[17] *Gosudarstvennaia Duma. Sbornik materialov*, No. 144.
[18] *GDSO. 1907 god. Sessia II*, I, 2125–26.

Democrat A. G. Zurabov leveled a strong attack against the army as unable to defend the country and capable only of serving the repressive domestic policies of the government. The outraged right wing of the Duma demanded the expulsion of the orator. Since the Duma was evenly divided and the Koło held the balance of power, F. A. Golovin, the president, consulted Dmowski. Dmowski replied evasively that the Koło did not wish to oppose the president and would not vote against a proposal for expulsion if it were presented by him but that the Poles did not desire to intervene in matters connected with the army and arouse a crisis. In the end, the Poles absented themselves from the session that discussed the matter.[19]

On the other hand, the issue of the budget expressed a system of government that was directed against Polish national interests but that could not be immediately replaced. Therefore, the Poles made it clear that they would vote for the budget only if the government showed a change in policy. Władysław Żukowski referred to the "parallel between political reaction and state capitalism," the latter characterized as the system of regulations and monopolies that created a budget independent of taxation and assessment. Jan Stecki asserted that "to vote the government credits means agreeing to its plans and actions while to deny it credits means compelling it to submit to the demands and directions of the people's representatives." He concluded that the task of the Duma was to deprive the government of those positions that allowed it to dream of taking the offensive.[20] According to Dmowski, the Poles

[19] "Zapiski F. A. Golovina," *Krasnyi arkhiv*, 19 (1926), 142–44; Alfred Levin, *The Second Duma* (New Haven, 1940), p. 298.

[20] *GDSO. 1907 god. Sessiia II*, I, 900, 907, 927; also, F. Dan, "Obshchaia politika pravitel'stva i izmenenia v gosudarstvennoi organizatsii v period 1905–1907 gg.," *Obshchestvennoe dvizhenie* (St. Petersburg, 1911), IV (2), 118.

made it known to the government that, in exchange for passage of the school bill, they would support the budget.[21] However, Stolypin's government felt strong enough not only to refuse concessions to the Poles but also to dissolve the Duma and, in the Manifesto of June 3, 1907, to alter the electoral law itself.

[21] Dmowski, *Niemcy,* pp. 118–19; *Polityka polska,* pp. 70–71.

IV

THE POLISH KOŁO AND NATIONALITY QUESTIONS

IN THE THIRD DUMA

THE ATTITUDE OF THE GOVERNMENT toward Russia's national minorities was demonstrated explicitly by the Manifesto of June 3, 1907, which stated that the State Duma "must be Russian in spirit" and that other nationalities "must not and shall not appear in a number giving them the possibility of being the controllers of purely Russian issues."[1] In conformity with this policy, 39 deputies out of a total of 442 represented the national minorities and, of these, the representation of the Poles in the Duma from the Kingdom was reduced to 11. Indeed, the Poles suffered the most by the new electoral law. Whereas, in European Russia, one member of the Duma represented a population of 240,000, in Poland the figure was now one representative for 750,000. Of the 11 Poles, 9 were National Democrats. Seven Polish delegates from the western Russian provinces composed the Polish-Lithuanian-Belorussian group which cooperated with the Koło. In the Duma as a whole, the new electoral law assured a predominance of conservative property owners. The opposition parties which had held the upper hand in the first two Dumas now played a secondary

[1] Lazarevskii, *Zakonodatel'nye*, pp. 557–58.

role. In the first session of the Third Duma, the Octobrists, who held 35 percent of the seats, numbered 154. The parties to the right of them comprised 51 Rightists, 26 Nationalists, and 70 Moderate Rightists. The parties to the left, numbering 141, included 54 Kadets and 28 Progressives.[2]

The first session of the Third Duma in November 1907 brought out clearly the attitudes of all sides toward the Polish question as well as the aspirations of the Polish delegation in the transformed Russian legislature. In the discussion on the drafting of the address to the throne, Dmowski expressed reservations because of an omission and made the modest proposal that the address include the phrase that "the Duma will devote itself to satisfying the legitimate strivings of the nationalities entering into the composition of the state." Although Miliukov had originally supported the Polish proposal and stated that "genuine patriotism should be Russian and not Great Russian patriotism,"[3] the Kadets finally voted for the Octobrist version of the address. The Polish suggestion was rejected by a large majority, and the Koło abstained from the voting.[4] The moderate-leftist Octobrist M. Ia. Kapustin observed that many of the claims of the nationalities were just, such as local self-government in Poland, but that there was no place for them in the address to the throne. However, those demands would be met in various acts of legislation. "We are not going backwards."[5] Count A. A. Uvarov, another Octobrist, also spoke of urban and rural self-government for Poland

[2] Mirosław Wierzchowski, "Sprawy polskie w III Dumie państwowej (1907–1912)," *Kwartalnik Historyczny*, 2 (1963), 405–407; Samuel N. Harper, *The New Electoral Law for the Russian Duma* (Chicago, 1908), p. 39; Alfred Levin, "June 3, 1907: Action and Reaction," *Essays in Russian History*, ed. Alan D. Ferguson and Alfred Levin (Hamden, Conn., 1964), pp. 252–55, 272.

[3] *GDSO. 1907–1908 gg. Sessiia I* (St. Petersburg, 1908), I, 149–51.

[4] *Ibid.*, pp. 162–63.

[5] *Ibid.*, pp. 172–73.

"but obviously on the condition that the borderlands do not demand what the central parts of Russia do not have."[6] In his opening address to the Duma on November 16, Prime Minister Stolypin spoke of projects for self-government in certain border areas of the Empire, but "the government will be directed by the idea of the unity and integrity of the state."[7] In reply, Dmowski referred to the altered conditions of legislative work and avoided the problem of autonomy. His reference to Polish demands that had been made during the period of the first two Dumas but that could no longer be met immediately, as well as demands that could never be realized, brought cheers from the center and right. Addressing himself to Stolypin's remarks, Dmowski asked whether the government had in mind the continuation of "a purely bureaucratic administration in the country" or "genuinely broad self-government with an invitation to the forces of society to fill those lacunae of state life that the bureaucracy has been unable to fill." In regard to the reduction of the number of deputies in the Duma from Poland, Dmowski remarked that this change testified that the government was determined not to follow a new path. It intended to pursue in relation to the borderlands a traditional policy whereby the inhabitants, like those of Poland, would be considered "second-class citizens of this state." In conclusion, he asserted that the Poles would never reconcile themselves to such a position and that the Koło did not see in Stolypin's declaration hope for a "genuine renewal of the structure of state" and, particularly, for those reforms necessary for Poland.[8]

In a second address on the same day, November 16,

[6] *Ibid.*, pp. 420–21.
[7] *Ibid.*, p. 311.
[8] *Ibid.*, pp. 337–43.

Stolypin replied energetically to Dmowski's demand that the government rely not on bureaucratic centralization but on local self-government. He stated that although the government did not object to cooperating with local elements, "the force of self-government on which the government will rely must always be a national force." He charged that the Poles, who had just called themselves second-class citizens, were such because they refused to use Russian as the language of state in any institution of higher learning in Poland. This was Stolypin's reply to the Polish charge that there were proportionately fewer schools in Poland in 1900 than there had been before 1830. The Poles, he declared, should ask for political decentralization only after they had become part of the general national "cement." Decentralization could come only from an "excess of strength." If it should be demanded in a time of weakness in order to break the ties that ought to bind the borderlands to the center, "the government will reply: No!" Stolypin concluded by urging the Poles to share the Russian point of view and recognize that the "highest blessing" was to be a Russian citizen, after which all rights would be received and the Poles might call themselves first-class citizens. Since local agencies in Russia had always "borne official state duties," all reforms, in order to be vital, had to draw their strength from "national Russian principles."[9]

Following Stolypin's address, and throughout the sessions of the Duma, the Poles were subjected to vitriolic attacks by deputies of the Rightist and Moderate Rightist parties. Among them were N. E. Markov, V. M. Purishkevich, and G. G. Zamyslovskii, "the three principal spokesmen of reaction." Markov, "the monotonous spokesman . . . of subsided opinion," was "commonplace and vulgar," and Zamyslov-

[9] *Ibid.*, pp. 352–53.

skii, a public prosecutor from Vilno, was "a renegade Liberal, rather a slippery politician."[10] Zamyslovskii was "an important figure" in the Ministry of Justice where he had "ties" with the reactionary minister, I. G. Shcheglovitov.[11] The "recklessly inflammatory" Purishkevich, the most ardent and die-hard monarchist in the Duma, was "a dangerous little man with a remarkable gift of abusive oratory."[12] Other figures were Eulogius, the Orthodox Bishop of Chełm, "a politician bishop," and the Rightist expert on Polish matters, S. N. Alekseev, the Russian delegate to the Duma from Warsaw. Alekseev published *Golos Rusi*, which was subsidized by the government.[13] In various statements, Purishkevich rejected the idea that Russia wanted Polish "servility" but recalled 1830 and 1863 and warned that any desire for autonomy was "to nurse dreams." Alekseev considered Purishkevich too moderate and charged that the entire nineteenth century had been devoted by the Poles to the effort "to call back to life from beyond the grave the ghost of the Polish state." The desire of the Koło for autonomy was neither more nor less than a step toward the independence of Poland, and the use of the term "decentralization" was simply a ruse. Zamyslovskii conceded that Dmowski's plea for decentralization signified less than autonomy but contended that it meant more than the self-government offered by the government, which also had in mind guarantees for Russian rights and the Russian language. Zamyslovskii also attacked Polish "religious fanaticism" and spoke of the need to strengthen the "Russian"

---

[10] Bernard Pares, *My Russian Memoirs* (London, 1931), pp. 148, 174.
[11] *Padenie tsar'skogo rezhima* (Moscow-Leningrad, 1924–1927), III, 353.
[12] Richard Charques, *The Twilight of Imperial Russia* (London, 1965), pp. 168–69.
[13] *Padenie tsar'skogo rezhima*, III, 109, 112.

population of the nine western provinces against "foreign (*inorodcheskii*) separatism."[14]

Speaking for the members of the Koło, Ludomir Dymsza commented that Stolypin's declaration was one of the "old songs" about "mature political thought" and the "strong will of the state." In drawing the distinction between citizenship and nationality, he argued that the Poles were being offered the right to become Russian citizens without the right of nationality. Żukowski stated that the Poles were genuine nationalists, respected the national sensibilities of their opponents, and would never offend Russian feelings of patriotism and religion.[15]

As spokesman for the influential Octobrists, Uvarov promised the Poles "with great satisfaction" everything that the central Russian provinces enjoyed along the lines of broad urban and rural self-government "but, of course, subject to the condition that the borderlands by no means demand what the central parts of Russia do not have." He suggested that the Poles were making a mistake by characterizing themselves as second-class citizens. "We wish, of course, to see them as first-class citizens, but I must say that we Russian citizens cannot give them any other first-class rights than the rights of first-class Russian citizens, and certainly not citizens of a Polish kingdom."[16]

The first specific issue connected with the nationality question to be considered by the Duma was the bill presented by the government on November 16 to introduce the teaching of Polish and arithmetic in Polish in the normal schools of Chełm and Biała Podlaska and to create official positions for teachers of Polish in five other normal schools

---

[14] *GDSO. 1907–1908 gg. Sessiia I,* I, 379–85, 411–18, 474–79.
[15] *Ibid.,* pp. 451–53, 558–61.
[16] *Ibid.,* pp. 420–21.

and of Lithuanian in one other.[17] The issue was sensitive because Chełm and Biała Podlaska were located in the ethnically mixed Polish-Ukrainian borderland between the Bug and Wieprz rivers within the Congress Kingdom. The report of the Duma's committee on education referred to the laws of June and October 1905 allowing the limited use of Polish in the elementary schools of Poland and noted that the bill was primarily concerned with the training of teachers. Approval was recommended. The reporter, E. P. Kovalevskii, an Octobrist, explained that the teaching of Polish in the normal schools would not be obligatory but would be for persons of Polish nationality and "for those desiring it."[18]

Although the bill concerned a strictly local matter, it immediately aroused the nationalist indignation of the right. During the first reading, Eulogius expressed "anxiety" over the fate of the Russian state schools in Poland and fear that the bill was "a certain infringement of the rights of this school system, a new step towards its Polonization." He contended that teaching in the state schools everywhere in the Empire should be in Russian just as in America where, despite its mixture of nationalities, public schools conducted instruction only in English.[19] On the other hand, Uvarov supported the bill as a "practical" measure. "I believe that all Russians wishing to be useful in Russian affairs in Poland ought to understand Polish." V. K. Von Anrep seconded him and declared Octobrist support for the bill.[20]

In national questions, the center Octobrists, as represented by Guchkov and Von Anrep, tended to go along with the right in matters of political nationalism, such as the

[17] *Gosudarstvennaia Duma. Prilozheniia k stenograficheskim otchetam gosudarstvennoi Dumy. Tretii sozyv. 1907–1908 gg. Sessiia I* (St. Petersburg, 1908), I, No. 82, pp. 339–41.
[18] *GDSO. 1907–1908 gg. Sessiia I,* I, 1548–51.
[19] *Ibid.*, pp. 1511–53.
[20] *Ibid.*, pp. 1563–64, 1564–67.

curial system for the western zemstvos or prohibitions on the use of local languages in local courts or political restraints on Jews. On the other hand, they were inclined to side with parties to the left in questions of cultural nationalism, especially the use of native languages in the schools.[21]

Eulogius was able to substitute for the phrase, "for those desiring it," that of "should there be those desiring it." However, during the second reading, Kovalevskii pointed out that since the possibility existed, in Eulogius' version, that no one would want Polish, the credits for the teaching positions would have to be eliminated from the bill. In addition, the article dealing with the two normal schools would also have to be deleted, at least until the school population had been consulted. Eulogius' proposal was rejected and the bill passed on February 12, 1908.[22] However, despite the seeming unimportance of the school bill, the forces of the right also took issue with it in the State Council. A. S. Stishinskii and P. N. Durnovo led the offensive. Durnovo, who immediately related the language question to the issue of the separation of Chełm from Poland, rejected "cosmopolitan theories" concerning the freedom supposedly to be enjoyed by other languages. A national policy had to be pursued by "the most direct route," and obstacles on the way had to be brushed aside. Such a policy demanded "firmness and perhaps severity," and it was impossible to be firm by trying to satisfy everyone. If Chełm had to be Russian "for the higher needs of state policy," and if children learned arithmetic badly because it was taught in Russian, "this is not a great harm."[23] Witte re-

[21] "Natsionalisticheskie i natsional'nie techeniia v tret'ei Dume," *Russkaia mysl'*, 8 (1912), 2123.

[22] *GDSO. 1907–1908 gg. Sessiia I*, I, 1667, 1775–78, 1794.

[23] *Gosudarstvennyi Sovet. Stenograficheskie otchety* (hereafter cited as *GSSO*). *1907–1908 gg. Sessiia III* (St. Petersburg, 1908), pp. 667–68.

marked that when he had been a member of the Council of Ministers, it had been resolved that "no substantial concessions" could be made to Poland, only minor ones, particularly the limited use of Polish in the schools. Also, the bill was not such as to make it "desirable" to collide with the Duma. Consequently, he supported the measure.[24] The State Council finally passed the bill on March 28, 1908, after having deleted the section on the teaching of arithmetic in Polish in the two normal schools.[25] This version was eventually approved by the Duma on April 30, 1909.[26]

The discussion of the budget of the Ministry of the Interior in April and May 1908 included debates of a general character on the Polish question. Upon taking the floor, Dmowski attacked the government strongly and was answered by Alekseev and Makarov, the "dense and arrogant"[27] assistant minister of the interior.[28] Dmowski characterized the struggle of the Russian bureaucracy in Poland with Polish nationalism as a failure, while Makarov referred to the existence of "exceptional measures" in Poland which could not be lifted "prematurely." He also defended martial law because of the "striving of Polish nationalists for separation from Russia."[29] Uvarov, who was charged with replying to Makarov on behalf of the Octobrists, stated that the Octobrists favored strong measures against revolution. On the other hand, "we have never wished to repress the borderlands; we will never follow that path on which the extreme rightists wish to lead us." He asserted that the Octobrists desired to grant Poland self-

[24] *Ibid.*, pp. 670, 684.
[25] *Ibid.*, pp. 810–11.
[26] *GDSO. 1908–1909 gg. Sessiia II* (St. Petersburg, 1909), IV, 298.
[27] Charques, *The Twilight of Imperial Russia*, p. 190.
[28] G. G. Zamyslovskii, *Pol'skii vopros v gosudarstvennoi Dume 3-go sozyva, 1-i sessii* (Vilno, 1909), p. 22.
[29] *GDSO. 1907–1908 gg. Sessiia I*, II, 2432–47, 2621–32.

government and responded with complete sympathy to the just demands of the Polish nation, "to the extent that these just demands are not at variance with the desires and rights of the Russian people."[30]

Dmowski's reply to Makarov constituted the clearest exposition so far of the program and aspirations of the Koło. It outlined the minimal concessions that the Poles expected from the government, even under the system of June 3, in return for Polish loyalty.[31] Dmowski distinguished between an opponent of the government and an enemy of the state. He denied as false the statement that the Poles were striving to separate the Kingdom from Russia. In his attack on the repressive measures of the government in Poland, he asked the Duma to look at the Polish question from the viewpoint of the interests of the Russian nation and state but not from that of the interests of the Russian bureaucracy in the borderlands. He rejected the charge that the Poles wanted either autonomy or nothing. While admitting that autonomy was desirable from the Polish view, Dmowski conceded that political conditions had altered considerably and that the Poles would accept "broad reforms." In the light of the fact that the Polish proposal for autonomy had been refused, "we will accept any good reform in the Kingdom of Poland. . . . We even agree that it is necessary to move gradually." Dmowski accepted Uvarov's statements that the Polish question be considered not from the position of Polish national interests but exclusively from that of a healthy understanding of Russian state interests. But he asked Uvarov whether the Octobrists "are really prepared to give what you yourselves have" in the way of education, courts, and administrators.

[30] *Ibid.*, pp. 2668–74.
[31] Mirosław Wierzchowski, *Sprawy Polski w III i IV Dumie Państwowej* (Warsaw, 1966), p. 77.

Finally, Dmowski asserted that the Koło was not bound
to any political party within the Duma but merely supported those programs and individuals that were sym-
pathetic to the Polish nation. "If more of such individuals
are found within the Russian opposition rather than in the
circle of official Russian patriots, it is not our fault."[32] In
brief, Dmowski abandoned the formula of political autonomy for Poland, insisted on the loyalty and moderation
of the Poles, and voiced the willingness of his countrymen
to accept any reforms and improvements in Poland. He
opened the door to the cooperation of the Koło with the
Octobrists as the dominant political grouping in the Duma
and the one that offered the most sanguine expectations for
alleviating the situation of the Poles in the Empire.

In this connection, the report of the budget committee
of the Duma included a proposal introduced by the Octobrists and Moderate Rightists that, in the nine western
Russian provinces, the nobility elect its own marshals, as
was the practice in central Russia. Such an innovation
would constitute an improvement over the existing system
of appointment by the government.[33] This proposal was
firmly opposed by the Rightists. Purishkevich spoke of it as
"the first stone in the realization of the idea of autonomy"
and warned of "separatist tendencies" that might lead to
another uprising. Consequently, the Rightists regarded the
measure as "risky in the highest degree."[34] S. E. Kryzhanovskii, the "methodical and versatile"[35] assistant minister of
the interior and the author of the first draft of the electoral
law of June 3, considered the proposal "premature." He
raised the danger of handing over the entire local adminis-

[32] GDSO. 1907–1908 gg. Sessiia I, II, 2705–11.
[33] Gosudarstvennaia Duma. Doklady biudzhetnoi kommissii. Tretii
sozyv. Sessiia I. 1907–1908 gg. (St. Petersburg, 1908), p. 908.
[34] GDSO. 1907–1908 gg. Sessiia I, II, 2797–98.
[35] Charques, The Twilight of Imperial Russia, p. 172.

tration to the Polish nobility and, with regard to the consequences of the revolution of 1863, "we cannot say that they have disappeared completely and without a trace."[36] As a result of this strong reaction, the Octobrists and Moderate Rightists altered their proposal to one that replaced elections of the nobility by a formula connecting elections with the introduction of elective zemstvos in the indicated provinces "on the condition, however, of the protection of the interests of the Russian population in the area." This formula was approved.[37]

The Poles' policy of moderation and good will was a demanding one, and even earlier in the session the extreme difficulties they faced were shown in their sharp conflict with the Octobrists. The latter's general theoretical sympathy with the cultural nationalism of the Poles quickly passed into political hostility, for the Octobrist program was characterized by strong Great Russian nationalism, and it was essentially impossible for the Octobrists to distinguish sharply between political and cultural nationalism. The specific issue occurred in March 1908 when a 6.9 million ruble credit for elementary education was discussed as part of a program of universal elementary education.

Speaking for the Koło, Antoni Rząd called for the response of the schools to "the needs of the nationalities" and to "the language of the students." The existing school structure in Poland meant that the credits would not meet the genuine needs of mass education but would merely serve the government, "which has transformed the schools into a weapon of political propaganda." On the other hand, since the measure would benefit Russia proper, the Koło would not vote against it but would abstain from the vote.[38]

36 *GDSO. 1907–1908 gg. Sessiia I*, II, 2798–2801.
37 *Ibid.*, p. 2802; also Zamyslovskii, *Pol'skii vopros*, pp. 52–53.
38 *GDSO. 1907–1908 gg. Sessiia I*, II, 522–23.

Rodichev, the fiery Kadet whose "whole mentality was the purest English liberalism of the fighting period,"[39] warned against "national prejudice" and the denial of local languages in instruction. By contrast, Eulogius took issue with both Rząd and Rodichev and insisted that the schools should not be a weapon of politics but must be "severely national," because one of their principal purposes was not only to teach, but also "to cultivate worthy Russian citizens."[40]

The Octobrist position was defined by Von Anrep, the chairman of the school committee. He admitted that instruction in elementary schools should be in the native language but, at the same time, he emphasized that the "state language" had to be taught everywhere, even in Polish schools, and that it could do no harm or "corrupt the soul" of the students, as Rząd had asserted. He expressed indignation at the "insolent" position of the Koło and reproached the Poles for abstaining from the vote and being willing to let Russia "rot" in ignorance. Significantly, he added, "I am happy that we are in such a position that the voices of the representatives of the Polish provinces are not of decisive importance."[41] In reply, Dmowski observed that "if we have no reason for love, let us remember that the awakening of hatred leads to nothing good." He pointed out that, unlike Russia, Poland did not have zemstvos that would properly control the schools and that the credits would be used in Poland "against the aspirations of society" and in order "to harm us." He closed by supporting Rząd's statement on the voting and by referring to the "patience" of the Poles.[42]

Similarly, when the budget of the Holy Synod was being

[39] Pares, *My Russian Memoirs*, p. 89.
[40] *GDSO. 1907–1908 gg. Sessiia I*, II, 469–70, 534–36.
[41] *Ibid.*, pp. 547–49.
[42] *Ibid.*, pp. 664–67.

discussed in March, Dymsza accused the Synod of using funds for political aims. Specifically, the sums spent in Chełm were proportionately larger than elsewhere. Also, large church organizations and church schools were being maintained in Poland where the number of Orthodox was slight. The Poles were again going to abstain from the voting. They were naturally obliged to react negatively to the activity of the Holy Synod in Poland as being directed against Poland's religious and national interests. However, since there were no special credits for use in Poland, the Poles did not wish to oppose the allocation of funds for Russia's own religious needs.[43]

Shortly later, in June, during discussion of the budget of the Ministry of Education, Dmowski spoke out more sharply and attacked the ministry's activities in Poland where the schools were in "complete disorder." He declared that the state schools were in fact police schools and that their attempts at Russification were fruitless; the schools simply constituted an arena of conflict between student and teacher which gave rise to pathological hatred and irritation that were objectively harmful to Russian interests of state. Predictably, Dmowski was attacked by the right and defended by Rodichev, who protested against forcing the Russian language on the Poles.[44] The policy of the Octobrists in this matter of nationalism and education remained "extremely vacillating."[45] Von Anrep attacked at great length the inadequacies of the Ministry of Education and demanded the creation of a school system that would arouse "feelings of conscious patriotism and national pride." However, "by patriotism we do not mean chauvinism," and

---

[43] *Ibid.*, pp. 835–41.

[44] *GDSO. 1907–1908 gg. Sessiia I*, III, 2469–83, 2772–74.

[45] *Tret'ia gosudarstvennaia Duma. Materialy dlia otsenki ee deiatel'nosti* (St. Petersburg, 1912), p. 136.

the schools must be "the propagator of broad national tolerance and justice."[46] Furthermore, a group of Kadets and Octobrists, including Von Anrep and Uvarov, introduced a motion in the debate on the budget of the Ministry of Education that demanded a fundamental school reform in Poland where the system did not respond either to the interests of the state or the cultural and national needs of the population. However, in order to appease the right, the name of the "Kingdom of Poland" was replaced by that of "Warsaw Educational District." This displeased the Koło and, in the end, the amendment was postponed, to await "more favorable circumstances."[47]

Although the first session of the third Duma accomplished next to nothing on the Polish question, Dmowski and the Koło persevered in their policy of restraint and moderation. The earlier demand for autonomy was not revived, and expectations remained confined to smaller concessions, especially in the areas of education and self-government. Much weight was attributed to Uvarov's statements suggesting the grant to the Poles of the rights and privileges enjoyed in Russia proper. In addition, the hope persisted that, despite the action of the government on June 3 and despite the strong element of nationalism that was a necessary cement of the Octobrist party, the center parties of the Duma would both satisfy legitimate and minimal Polish desires and also further the recovery and stability of the entire Empire on a basis of legality and parliamentary responsibility. In this context, the Koło endorsed the candidacy of the Octobrist N. A. Khomiakov for the office of president of the Duma. It also supported Stolypin's program of agrarian reform based on the decree of November 9, 1906, that was designed to liquidate the

[46] *GDSO. 1907–1908 gg. Sessiia I*, III, 2398–2401.
[47] Wierzchowski, *Sprawy Polski*, p. 80.

Russian commune. Furthermore, in opposition to the leftist parties in the Duma, the Koło voted in favor of an Octobrist motion to limit each speech on the agrarian reform measure to ten minutes.[48]

During the second reading of the agrarian bill, in February 1909, Władysław Grabski introduced a motion that in Poland rural communes be granted the right to consolidate field strips on the basis of a favorable vote of two-thirds of the members of the commune rather than, as heretofore, by a unanimous vote. Grabski's proposal was supported by the committee reporter, S. I. Shidlovskii, and was accepted by the Duma.[49] It eventually passed into law in 1910 as the only legislation of the Third Duma that had a substantive effect in Poland. The conservative *Novoe vremia* commented on the Polish vote in favor of the agrarian reform: "This is the first serious manifestation by the Poles of their readiness to work hand in hand with the Russian government in matters of social significance to the entire state."[50]

The Poles also voted for a bill introduced by Stolypin on the basis of which persons indicted for political disloyalty or placed under police surveillance might not perform military service. The vote was characterized by the official organ *Rossiia* as "the first symptom of the sobering up of the Poles."[51] The Kadet newspaper *Rech'* labeled the Polish vote a "disgraceful" manifestation of nonsolidarity with the progressive elements of the Russian population.[52] However, *Rech'* also quoted the Octobrist leader Guchkov as asserting that "relations with the Poles are improving. They have started on the road of a realistic policy and hope exists for the possibility of common work with them. In view of

[48] *GDSO. 1908–1909 gg. Sessiia II* (St. Petersburg, 1909), I, 1224–25.
[49] *Ibid.*, pp. 857–61.
[50] *Novoe vremia*, Nov. 19, 1908.
[51] *Rech'*, Nov. 15, 1908.
[52] *Ibid.*, Nov. 20, 1908.

this, the Octobrists must meet them and grant the local self-government which we ourselves possess."[53]

However, the further course of the Third Duma demonstrated that Polish amenability and Octobrist promises led to few tangible results. Specifically, the ministerial crisis of 1908–1909 and the general intensification of nationalist policies that followed in both the government and the legislature darkened whatever possibilities had existed for an amelioration of the conditions of the Poles within the Empire. As the elements of political reaction recovered strength after 1907, they directed their main efforts against the head of the government, Stolypin, who was a firm adherent of the new constitutional structure. At the same time, Guchkov's exposures in the Duma of Russian military incompetence and his demands for a thorough reform of the system embarrassed Stolypin and aroused the ire of the court camarilla.

The first legislative crisis was provoked by the bill for the lists of a Naval General Staff, the passage of which by the Duma was attacked by the right as an infringement of the prerogatives of the emperor. The crisis lasted from July 1908, when the bill was rejected by the State Council, to April 1909, when the bill was vetoed by the emperor after the State Council had been induced to ratify it under strong pressure from the cabinet. Although Stolypin remained in office, his authority was gravely weakened by Nicholas' decision. Stolypin's working alliance with the Octobrists was strained, and the forces of reaction were strengthened by success.[54] The consequence was that Stolypin was obliged to lay greater emphasis on a program of nationalism, always a strong element in his outlook. Furthermore,

[53] *Ibid.*, Nov. 18, 1908.
[54] For details, see my article, "Stolypin and the Russian Ministerial Crisis of 1909," *California Slavic Studies*, 4 (1967), 1–38.

the broad Octobrist center, a loose union of interest groups, found difficulty in maintaining cohesion on the issue of nationalism. In addition, while the government at first had relied on a combination of Octobrists and Moderate Rightists, in the third session of the Duma, during the autumn of 1909, it began to sponsor a rightist bloc. This bloc comprised the Rightists, the new Russian National party that had been formed in October from the union of the former Nationalists and the Moderate Rightists, and the Right Octobrists, who had left the main party in May 1909.[55] This rightist grouping also had the sympathy of a significant number of Octobrists in matters of nationalism.[56] In voting strength, the Octobrists dropped from 154 in the first session of the Third Duma to 121 in the fifth session, while the 147 members of the Rightist, Nationalist, and Moderate Rightist parties increased to the number of 156 the members of the parties to the right of the Octobrists in 1911–1912.[57]

In this altered situation, the Koło's expectations of cooperation with the Octobrist center and of the latter's support faced possible frustration. Within the Koło there developed opposition to the policy of compromise with the Octobrists on the grounds that there was no hope of changing the policy of the government. This internal discord resulted in the resignation from the Duma in January 1909 of Dmowski. He had opposed any alterations in tactics, had retained confidence in the constitutionalism of the Octobrists, and had insisted that Poland's daily interests be de-

[55] P. N. Miliukov, "Politicheskie partii v gosudarstvennoi Dume za piat' let," *Ezhegodnik gazety Rech' na 1912 god* (St. Petersburg, 1912), pp. 79–81.
[56] A. S. Izgoev, "Ot tret'ei Dumy k chetvertoi," *Ezhegodnik gazety Rech' na 1913 god* (St. Petersburg, 1913), pp. 186–87.
[57] *Gosudarstvennaia Duma. Obzor deiatel'nosti gosudarstvennoi Dumy tret'iago sozyva 1902–1912 gg.* (St. Petersburg, 1912), I, Prilozhenie 4 (a), 98–99.

fended in the Duma.[58] A personal factor in Dmowski's decision may have been that "his dictatorial tendencies" had alienated in his party "even those who shared his views."[59] In general, however, the Poles did not depart from their policy of protesting injustices and requesting moderate concessions. The Koło supported the opposition in the affair of Evno Azev, the double-dealing revolutionary and police agent. It demanded the elimination of exceptional regulations and restrictions on civil rights, and it left the chamber in protest against the proposal of the government to cut short the debate. It also went along with the Octobrists when, against the wishes of the government and the rightist parties, they liberalized certain religious bills that increased official religious tolerance. On the other hand, the Koło, in opposition to the left, voted in favor of the agrarian legislation based on the decree of November 9, 1906, that had little significance in Poland where peasant property was in private hands.[60]

During the discussion in March of the budget of the Ministry of Justice for 1909, the Koło took the initiative and attempted to obtain wider access for Poles to judicial appointments in the Kingdom. Dymsza introduced a motion that Polish nationality should not be an obstacle to such appointments. The immediate hue and cry aroused on the right was demonstrated by Zamyslovskii, who cynically declared that the Kingdom of Poland had "come and gone" (*bylo da splylo*). He pointed out that there was no Kingdom of Poland, only the provinces of the Vistula which, furthermore, had no autonomy. Consequently, the appointment of provincial officials there was simply an administra-

[58] Kukiel, *Dzieje Polski porozbiorowe*, pp. 480–81; Wierzchowski, *Sprawy Polski*, pp. 118–19.
[59] *Rech'*, Jan. 26, 1909.
[60] Wierzchowski, "Sprawy polskie," p. 413.

tive matter that did not concern the Duma.[61] The Octobrist
N. P. Shubinskii also criticized Dymsza's proposal as "uto-
pian" and expressed the view that the Poles' attitude toward
Russian judges was one of "complete respect."[62] However,
the culminating point of the discussion was the declaration
of the minister of justice, Shcheglovitov. He denied that in
Poland courts composed of Poles were "desirable and necessary." Communal (*gmina*) courts were in Polish hands and
had been unable to control the revolutionary situation in
1905 when "the national separatist movement" had gained
control of them. Therefore, the regular courts, which were
"fortunately" staffed by Russians, should not be opened
to Poles who would "obstruct the courts by their separatist policy" and loosen the "unbreakable tie" that must
exist between Poland and the other parts of the Russian
Empire.[63]

Dymsza's motion was defeated by thirty votes, with both
the Rightists and Social Democrats united in opposition to
it, but the Koło still voted in favor of the budget of the
Ministry of Justice.[64] However, dissatisfaction in Poland
obliged the Koło to reply later in the month to Shcheglovitov. Żukowski took issue with the minister's remarks, particularly the latter's use of the word "obstruct." Von Anrep
stated that the nationality question raised by Żukowski was
"untimely" and that the Octobrists would at some time ex-
press their position on the subject of the borderlands "on
the basis of a just recognition of genuinely honest national
and cultural needs." This vague and circumspect comment
provoked derision from the right. Purishkevich shouted

---

[61] *GDSO. 1908–1909 gg. Sessiia II*, II, 2948–52.

[62] *Ibid.*, p. 2943.

[63] *Ibid.*, pp. 2914–24. When questioned after the March Revolution
whether he could provide facts regarding the separatist activity of Polish
judges, Shcheglovitov gave no reply. *Padenie tsar'skogo rezhima*, II, 370.

[64] *GDSO. 1908–1909 gg. Sessiia II*, II, 2961.

from his place, "Ask the right wing of your party," and Markov exclaimed, "Your strength is not up to the task."[65] In
reply, Miliukov attacked Shcheglovitov's insulting speech
as an "anti-patriotic act," and, since the minister had made
it clear that his words were not his personal opinion but an
expression of the policy of the entire cabinet, the Kadet
leader charged that the cabinet had to bear the responsibility for an anti-national policy.[66]

The first gain made by the Koło in the Third Duma was
in an area of taxation not closely related to the sensitive
issue of nationalism. In September 1909, a bill was introduced by the Ministry of Finance to alter the method of
taxing real estate. The existing system assessed a total sum
for the entire state that was then apportioned among the
several provinces. The bill proposed to assess the income on
real estate at 6 percent of the value with an annual tax of
.3 percent on the income. The reform was to apply to Poland, although the zemstvo institution of self-government
did not function there and the reform would have to be
carried out by the unsympathetic Russian bureaucracy.[67]
The Poles strongly supported the bill because it introduced
in Poland a tax rate the same as that for the central Russian
provinces. The bill was very much in line with the type of
modest and realistic reform espoused by the Koło. The bill
aroused lively polemics during the plenary debates. Extreme Rightists attacked the principle of equal taxation for
Poland and Russia on the grounds of the privileged economic position of the former with regard to the vast Russian
market. The industry, railways, and cities of the Kingdom
were developing rapidly, thanks to a protective tariff policy
and receptive Russian markets; moreover, the Rightists

[65] GDSO. 1908–1909 gg. Sessiia II, III, 1136–37.
[66] Ibid., pp. 1141–42.
[67] GDSO. 1909–1910 gg. Sessiia III (St. Petersburg, 1910), I, 2250–57.

claimed, Polish agriculture found an outlet in the Russian army stationed in Poland. Therefore, the Rightists suggested that property income in Poland be assessed at the level of 10 percent rather than 6 percent. It was even pointed out that, since Poland was a conquered colony and since all states exploited their colonies, Russia should do the same without restraint and should abandon a policy of developing its border areas at its own expense.[68]

Two representatives of the Koło, Żukowski and Grabski, replied to the Rightists and pointed out that the statements concerning Poland's economically preferential relationship to Russia were inexact and actually applied to the period ten to twenty years earlier. Since that time, vast changes had occurred. The cultivation of cotton in Turkestan and the simultaneous increase in import duties were favoring the Moscow textile industry over that of Łódź. The Kingdom received no budgetary allocations but contributed fifteen million rubles annually to the treasury. It also occupied last place in railroad development. Although the industry of Baku and the Don basin was evolving more rapidly than that of Poland, there was no proposal to increase the former's tax rate. Inasmuch as Poland had no separate treasury after 1867, it should not pay separate and higher taxes.[69]

The Poles were supported in their arguments by the Kadets and Progressives, but the Octobrists accepted a proposal to retain in Poland the tax rate of 10 percent on the condition that 40 percent of the tax on property should be used for local needs. After the introduction into Poland of institutions of urban self–government, the tax structures

[68] *Ibid.*, pp. 2333–39, 2353–54; *GDSO. 1909–1910 gg. Sessiia III*, II, 981–94, 999–1002, 1016–28.
[69] *GDSO. 1909–1910 gg. Sessiia III*, I, 2347–51, 2369–74; *GDSO. 1909–1910 gg. Sessiia III*, II, 1002–11.

of the Kingdom and the central Russian provinces were to become uniform. In this version, the bill was passed by a majority over the opposition of the right.[70] Although it was the first concrete gain of the Koło in the Duma, the hesitant and reserved attitude of the Octobrist center toward positive concessions to the Poles was clearly revealed. Furthermore, the measure had no practical significance in that urban self-government was not introduced into Poland.

Octobrist ambiguities were also shown by the Opole church question. This issue demonstrated a weakening of the Octobrist position in the matter of freedom of conscience when Roman Catholicism was concerned. A contrast was also provided with the position taken by the Octobrists in May 1909 when they revised in a more liberal sense three bills introduced in the Duma by the government dealing with the removal of civil and political disabilities on persons giving up the priesthood, with the congregations of Old Believers, and with changes of faith.[71] In 1877, the Catholic church in the village of Opole had been closed during the period of Uniate persecutions. After the decree of religious tolerance in April 1905, a majority of the village inhabitants had returned to Catholicism and had requested the return of the church. They had been informed that the Duma would decide the issue but, in 1907, the governor of the province of Siedlce on his own initiative had handed the church over to the Orthodox clergy.[72]

In November 1908, the Koło introduced an interpellation and was confident of redress because of the obvious miscarriage of justice. However, this local incident provoked extended and acrimonious debate in which the ques-

[70] *Ibid.*, pp. 1011–28, 1040–47; *Gosudarstvennaia Duma. Obzor deiatel'nosti gosudarstvennoi Dumy tret'iago sozyva*, II, 140–44.

[71] For further details, see my article "Stolypin and the Ministerial Crisis of 1909," pp. 27–32.

[72] *GDSO. 1909–1910 gg. Sessiia III*, I, 424–34.

tion of Russo-Polish relations was carried into the area of religious antagonism. The government spokesman, A. N. Kharuzin, voiced the official position in January 1910 when he defended the right of the local Orthodox population to possession of the church. He declared that the Holy Synod did not deem it possible to return the church to the Catholic clergy, and he exonerated the provincial authorities by stating that the Ministry of the Interior had not informed them of the petition of the Opole Catholics.[73] The issue was then debated at six sessions of the Duma between January and March. The representative of the Rightists, Bishop Eulogius of Chełm, insisted that the Orthodox of the district were being persecuted by the Catholics, that the interpellation was intended to discredit the Orthodox clergy, and that the issue of the church was a religious pretext aimed at concealing political aims.

The Poles stated that in the district of Chełm the Orthodox clergy, with the cooperation of the administration, were persecuting the Catholics and forcibly appropriating the latter's churches. In the debate, the position of the Poles received unusually active support from the entire left wing of the Duma—Progressives, Kadets, the Labor Group, and the Social Democrats. All agreed in condemning the seizure of the church as an act of militant nationalism that would inflame Russo–Polish relations and as a useless and harmful political interference in religious affairs. The Kadet Rodichev protested the sanctioning by the Duma of the principle that church property might be alienated by a simple administrative act.[74] However, the hope of the Poles for the support of the Octobrists proved vain. No Octobrists spoke during the debates. Only at the last session, P. B. Kamenskii read a declaration in the name of the party stating that the

[73] *GDSO. 1909–1910 gg. Sessiia III,* II, 412–24.
[74] *Ibid.,* pp. 731–51, 2384–88, 2327–28.

government's explanation of the legality of the actions of the governor of Siedlce was adequate but that the principle of freedom of conscience ought to be maintained by the government. This formula was approved by the Duma over the votes of the opposition, the Kadets taxing the Octobrist statement for its "amazing hypocrisy."[75]

The second half of the existence of the Third Duma continued to be disturbed by Polish grievances in the field of education. However, as the parliamentary forces on the right gained in strength, and as the policy of official nationalism was intensified by the government after the ministerial crisis of 1909, the possibilities of redress were further reduced. The focus of the problem was the language of instruction in schools, specifically the use of Polish in the schools of the Kingdom. The principal debates occurred over the bill on the regulations for public elementary schools introduced in the Duma by the Ministry of Education on November 1, 1907. The bill was referred to the committee on education. Of the fifty-five members of the committee, twenty-seven were Rightists and priests.[76] A special subcommittee was established under the Octobrist D. A. Leonov to work out detailed rules on the language of instruction in schools with non-Russian (*inorodcheskie*) nationalities, but its recommendations were rejected by the committee because of "scarcely surmountable difficulties."[77] The subcommittee was then instructed to limit itself to the more advanced and compact nationalities.

The subcommittee's report, which proposed that use of the students' native language be allowed in the first four

[75] *Ibid.*, p. 2988; *Tret'ia gosudarstvennaia Duma. Materialy*, p. 65.
[76] *Tret'ia gosudarstvennaia Duma*, p. 368.
[77] Report of the committee on education in *Gosudarstvennaia Duma. Prilozheniia k stenograficheskim otchetam gosudarstvennoi Dumy. Tretii sozyv. 1909–1910 gg. Sessiia III* (St. Petersburg, 1910), II, No. 322, p. 46.

years of elementary school,[78] was also rejected since the committee found it impossible to establish "impartial criteria" in order to decide fairly which nationalities had the right to a more extensive use of their own languages in the schools.[79] As a result, the bill was presented to the Duma without any regulations for non-Russian schools. The purpose of the elementary schools was declared to be that of giving to the students "a religious-moral education" and developing in them "a love for Russia." Teachers were to be Russian subjects of the Orthodox faith. Instruction was to be in Russian. If the students did not speak Russian, the native language might be used for the first two years. From the beginning of the third year, Russian was to be used exclusively except for the teaching of religion and the native language. The teaching of Russian had to commence no later than the third month of the first year. In areas of the Empire where the population was predominantly non-Orthodox, the question of religious instruction was to be decided by the local school board. The chairman and members of the school boards were required to be Russian subjects, and the chairman and no fewer than half of the members had to be Orthodox.[80]

The bill was first discussed at the very beginning of the fourth session of the Duma, on October 15, 1910. Władysław Jabłonowski, the spokesman for the Koło, attacked the bill as "hostile" in its provisions affecting so-called foreigners among whom the Poles were "mechanically" included. He declared that "the interests of the state" were understood by the government as a struggle with the national, religious, and cultural individualities of the non-Russian

[78] *GDSO. 1910–1911 gg. Sessiia IV* (St. Petersburg, 1911), I, 109–14.
[79] *Prilozheniia k stenograficheskim otchetam. 1909–1910 gg.*, II, No. 322, p. 47.
[80] *Ibid.*, pp. 232–40, 251.

minorities and that the Poles regarded the bill as "the most harmful provocation."[81] The bill was then debated by articles, those dealing with the language of instruction arousing the stormiest reactions. A proposal by Stanisław Maciejewicz that, in schools where the number of non-Orthodox students was no fewer than five, religious instruction be provided for their faith was rejected.[82] At this juncture, Leonov, in the name of the Octobrists, introduced a regulation for non-Russian schools that listed the nationalities whose languages might be used for instruction and extended the use beyond the two-year limit of the government's bill to the first four years. On the other hand, Russian had to be taught from the very beginning of instruction and in Russian after the first year.[83]

The assistant minister of education, L. A. Georgievskii, aligned himself with Alekseev, the representative of school Russifiers in Poland, and protested "in the most energetic fashion" against the proposal on the grounds that in "great, indivisible, unified Russia . . . there must be a single, universal, unifying Russian state language." The minister of education, L. A. Kasso, also took exception to the Octobrist proposal. In opposition to them, Wiktor Jaroński of the Koło referred to the "mythical significance" attributed to Russian as the state language.[84] The Octobrist regulation was voted with a few modifications as was the additional proposal that the phrase, teachers "of the Orthodox faith," be replaced by that "of the Christian faith." On the other hand, although the article that the chairman and no fewer than half of the members of school boards had to be Orthodox was rejected, 116 to 112, an amendment was voted that these functionaries in the nine western and southwestern

[81] *GDSO. 1910–1911 gg. Sessiia IV*, I, 215–22.
[82] *Ibid.*, p. 990.
[83] *Ibid.*, pp. 1008–13.
[84] *Ibid.*, pp. 1013–16, 1158–61, 1139–43.

provinces of Russia and the district of Chełm must be Orthodox. Also, a motion by the Poles that in Poland all subjects except the Russian language be taught in Polish in the fifth and sixth years as well was defeated, 133 to 110.[85]

On November 29, 1910, the bill was returned to the committee on education where the Octobrist regulation on elementary schools for non-Russian students was thrown out and the article requiring teachers to be of the Orthodox religion was restored.[86] The second reading by articles began on February 4, 1911, and was a repetition of the first. The restorations of the committee on education were defeated, and the amendments voted during the first reading, including the Octobrist school regulation for non-Russians, were approved.

During the debate, the Russian National party objected strongly to the encouragement of "foreign cultures at the expense of the Russian state principle." Its spokesman, P. N. Balashov, read a statement that "the expulsion of the state language from non-Russian schools as the language of instruction unconditionally contradicts the interests of the state," and the party withdrew from the debates. But the bill establishing regulations for elementary schools, including schools for non-Russian students, was passed.[87] This measure, "one of the few liberal projects of the Third Duma,"[88] was then sent to the unsympathetic State Council where it was considered in the spring of 1912. The article dealing with the language of instruction in areas where the entering students did not speak Russian aroused the greatest discussion. Despite the argument of Ignacy Szebeko, a

[85] *Ibid.*, pp. 1238–79, 1394, 1659–60, 1287.
[86] *Gosudarstvennaia Duma. Prilozheniia k stenograficheskim otchetam gosudarstvennoi Dumy. Tretii sozyv. 1910–1911 gg. Sessiia IV* (St. Petersburg, 1911), III, No. 99, pp. 69, 95.
[87] *GDSO. 1910–1911 gg. Sessiia IV*, II, 1190–1200, 1518.
[88] *Tret'ia gosudarstvennaia Duma. Materialy*, p. 378.

Pole, that the bill made extremely minor language concessions,[89] the Council's committee on education rejected the
provision of the Duma's bill allowing four years of instruction in the native language. It accepted the original
version of the Ministry of Education permitting two years,
after which only religion and the native language might be
taught in that language. This modification was accepted
by Kasso, who considered two years "the maximum period
of time" for the native language to be of assistance. From
the viewpoint of the government, further concessions were
"undesirable and unacceptable." The State Council passed
the two-year limit.[90] The bill was then sent to a joint commission, but no agreement was reached and the measure
was not taken up again by the Duma.[91]

In May 1911, the Duma considered a bill on higher elementary schools that were designed to serve as a link between primary and intermediary schools. The bill was
passed that month with certain changes in a nationalist
spirit. Jan Harusewicz of the Koło pointed out that the
greatest inadequacy of the bill was the obligatory teaching
of all subjects except religion and the native language of
non-Russians in Russian. Furthermore, there was no guarantee for religious instruction to non-Orthodox students if
they constituted fewer than half of the student body, and
the teaching of the native language was not obligatory. He
asserted that Polish should be the language of instruction
in the entire school system of Poland. Specifically, all subjects except the Russian language ought to be taught in
Polish. In addition, religious instruction should be given to
students of all faiths represented by at least one-quarter

[89] *GSSO. 1911–1912 gg. Sessiia VII* (St. Petersburg, 1912), p. 2740.
[90] *Ibid.*, pp. 2984, 3019–20, 3048.
[91] *Ibid.*, pp. 3864, 4702.

of the school enrollment. Alfons Parczewski proposed that the native language of a nationality be an obligatory subject for the students of that nationality if they constituted at least one-quarter of the student body.[92]

Von Anrep, the Octobrist reporter from the committee on education, rejected the Polish claims on the grounds of the "needs of the state." He also spoke of the need "to struggle with the longings of whole large masses surrounding Russia in a ring."[93] The motions of Harusewicz and Parczewski were defeated. Another motion by Harusewicz that the determination of the nationality of students belonged exclusively to their parents was likewise rejected by the Duma on the advice of Von Anrep, who claimed that the right to define the nationality of the students belonged to the school administration. Also, the Duma accepted the proposal of the Nationalist V. K. Tychinin that religion had to be taught in Russian to non-Orthodox students who were Russian, Russian being defined officially as Great Russian, Little Russian, and Belorussian.[94] In connection with an article of the bill allowing the teaching of local languages on a non-obligatory basis, a Polish proposal that the teaching of Polish in higher elementary schools in the Kingdom be obligatory for students of Polish nationality was defeated, 118 to 72. The Duma merely passed a motion of Harusewicz's allowing teaching of the local language to those students to whom it was native with the approval of the Ministry of Education.[95] The State Council revised the bill by excluding the provision for compulsory religious instruction for non-Orthodox students numbering more than a half of the school enrollment and by disallowing non-

[92] *GDSO. 1910–1911 gg. Sessiia IV*, III, 3549–54, 3558.
[93] *Ibid.*, pp. 3565, 3575.
[94] *Ibid.*, pp. 3568–69.
[95] *Ibid.*, pp. 3575–76.

Christian teachers. However, the joint commission restored the original version, which was accepted by both houses and received imperial confirmation in June 1912.[96]

Finally, the last session of the Third Duma debated and passed a bill introduced by the Ministry of Education to regulate private schools. This bill was liberalized considerably. Whereas the government's bill permitted instruction not in Russian only under certain circumstances and special conditions in areas of the country inhabited by non-Russians and exclusively for non-Russians, the Duma's committee on education broadened this concession. Whereas the ministerial bill conceded the right to establish private schools only to private individuals and organizations, the Duma extended this right to cities and zemstvo organizations. However, the committee's reporter, Leonov, recommended that an exception to this right be made of the cities in the nine western and southwestern provinces because the city administrations there were "predominantly in Polish hands." Consequently, the danger existed that the schools "would not meet the needs of the Russian population."[97] On the other hand, the committee proposed that the language of instruction be left to the founders, subject to the reservation that the Russian language be taught in Russian at all school levels, and that Russian history, geography, and literature be taught in Russian in elementary and intermediate schools. An exception to this provision was constituted again by the nine western and southwestern provinces as well as the Polish provinces of Lublin and Siedlce where Great Russians, Little Russians, and Belorussians who were non-Orthodox had to be taught in Russian in private schools.

[96] Gosudarstvennaia Duma. Obzor deiatel'nosti gosudarstvennoi Dumy tret'iago sozyva, II, pp. 456–57.
[97] GDSO. 1911–1912 gg. Sessiia V (St. Petersburg, 1912), IV, 1281–83.

The committee rejected the provisions of the ministerial bill that non-Orthodox individuals might establish schools exclusively for persons of their own religion, that Russian alone might be the language of instruction in advanced schools, and that all instruction had to be in Russian in schools with students of mixed nationalities. A concession that was regarded as of primary significance within Poland[98] was the recommendation of the committee on education that the teaching of Russian, history, geography, and literature be allowed by non-Russians.

As spokesman for the Poles, Harusewicz stated that the bill, despite its negative features, meant an improvement over existing conditions in the Kingdom of Poland, where education was subject to the arbitrariness and bureaucratic supervision of the Ministry of Education. Because it would introduce order into a situation of chaos, the Poles would vote for it. The committee version of the bill was strongly denounced by the Rightist Markov, who declared that any Jew could open a school and warned that the State Council would reject the bill "because there are individuals there of intelligence, experience, and, above all, love for the Russian people." The government insisted on its version. The assistant minister of education, M. A. Von Taube, rejected the committee alterations, including the language articles, and referred to the possibility of students' entering advanced schools without having an adequate knowledge of "the state language." However, the Duma passed the bill as emended by the committee on education on June 4, 1912.[99] The State Council actually passed the bill in 1913 but limited the use of the language of instruction by making Russian the compulsory language of instruction in schools

[98] *Siemieński, La Pologne,* p. 698.

[99] *GDSO. 1911–1912 gg. Sessiia* V, IV, 1283–85, 1296–1300, 1305–1306, 1319, 3429.

established by cities and zemstvo organizations. Despite this limitation, the Duma's committee on education recommended acceptance of the version of the bill passed by the State Council, and the bill was approved by the Duma on June 12, 1914.[100] Such were the extremely meager gains won by the Poles in the Duma in the vital area of education.

During the course of the fourth session of the Third Duma, the question of introducing zemstvo institutions into Poland was raised by the Octobrists. On the basis of the party's own program as well as the imperial edict of December 12, 1904, that spoke of expanding the activities of the zemstvos, seventy-eight Octobrists, led by Guchkov, submitted a proposal on November 12, 1910, that such local self-government be granted to Poland. However, this Octobrist action was in the nature of a *quid pro quo* inasmuch as the party was simultaneously supporting the proposal for the separation of Chełm from Poland in the form of a new Russian province. The reporter of the Duma's committee on local self-government, Leonov, presented the committee's findings on February 11, 1911. He referred to Alexander II's promise of self-government to the Poles in 1862. The revolt of 1863 had prevented any action from being taken. In 1864, the classless local commune (*gmina*) with limited powers had been introduced in the Kingdom. However, there remained the obvious and crying need for a broader structure of self-government with powers of taxation over larger areas. Therefore, the committee supported the application of the zemstvo regulations of 1890 to Poland on a classless basis as a "salutary reform."[101]

The chief of the Department for the Affairs of Local Economy, S. N. Gerbel, speaking for the minister of the

[100] *GSSO. 1912–1913 gg. Sessiia VIII* (St. Petersburg, 1913), pp. 1779–86, 2040; *GDSO. 1913–1914 gg. Sessiia II* (St. Petersburg, 1914), V, 1155.
[101] *GDSO. 1910–1911 gg. Sessiia IV*, IV, 1662–66.

interior, declared that the government had not renounced a zemstvo reform for Poland but that the issue was one of "extreme complexity" and the Octobrist proposal was "untimely." The related problem of urban self-government had to be taken into account, and there was the necessity of introducing simultaneously a uniform zemstvo tax structure in Poland where none yet existed. As a result, the creation of zemstvo institutions had to await a reform of the communal structure, which required detailed study. Gerbel was applauded on the right and by some benches in the center of the chamber.[102] The Rightist P. V. Berezovskii charged the Octobrists with dilatoriness in introducing their proposal as late as November 1910 if they thought it, as they alleged, such a pressing matter. He asserted that the real reason was their need for Polish support in the election of a new president of the Duma at the time when Khomiakov was being replaced by Guchkov. He also insisted that the proposal was being pushed at the moment because of the desire of the Octobrists to win the sympathy of liberal society in light of the forthcoming elections to the Fourth Duma. The Rightists opposed a zemstvo structure for all Poland because it would be dominated by the anti-Russian Polish intelligentsia and would consist of "revolutionary nests" that might bring about a repetition of 1830 and 1863. V. A. Bobrinskii, the Nationalist orator, stated that his party would support the Octobrists, but only on the condition that the Russian minority be protected. He also overtly connected the zemstvo issue with the question of Chełm, saying that no zemstvos ought to be established until that region had been separated from Poland.

Grabski angrily rejected the Rightist accusation of Polish disloyalty as groundless. In support of the Octobrist proposal, he pointed out that Poland received much less than

[102] *Ibid.*, pp. 1666–69.

its share of funds from taxation in matters of education and social welfare, largely owing to the absence of organs of local self-government to administer them. Miliukov stated that the Kadets would adhere to the proposal of the seventy-eight Octobrists, but he reproached the center for its faintheartedness. Referring to the Octobrist formula, "We will give you Poles what we ourselves have," he explained, "The formula was modest; its realization, as you know, has been even more modest." In conclusion, Leonov urged that the government ought to present its measures without delay. "This is one of the first links in that chain of cordial relations" that had to bind the Poles to Russia. The final vote of the Duma was to the effect that the submission of a bill by the government would be "desirable."[103]

Another proposal concerning Polish matters was introduced during the fifth session of the Duma. This was one to allow the sale of land in Poland from the large entailed estates of the Russian nobility. These estates had been created from imperial grants as a result of the confiscations of land from Polish landowners that had followed the suppression of the uprising of 1863. The Russian landowners were mostly absentee and had long been in the practice of leasing their land, very often to Jews.[104] Temporary regulations issued under Article 87 of the Fundamental Laws in 1906 were now to be made permanent. However, in order to prevent the bill's being used as a device by the Russian government to support the settlement of Russian peasants in Poland, the Octobrists in the Duma's land committee proposed that land from the estates be allowed to pass into the hands of "local" peasants "without distinction of faith and origin." The argument of Alekseev, the Russian deputy from Warsaw, that the word "local" would exclude Russian

[103] *Ibid.*, pp. 1670–76, 1676–77, 1677–82, 1687, 1691–92.
[104] *Rech'*, Feb. 26, 1913.

peasants and should be dropped from the bill was rejected by the Duma. The Poles supported the Octobrists, and the house accepted a modification proposed by Grabski that land might be acquired by other classes as well as peasants. The bill was strongly attacked by the right, and a representative of the Baltic German nobility warned of the danger of turning Russia into a "peasant state." Nevertheless, the Duma passed the committee version on May 19, 1912.[105]

During the fifth session of the Duma, much clamor was aroused by a bill introduced by the government for the purchase by the treasury of the Warsaw-Vienna railway line for 32 million rubles. Although the purchase was officially justified by strategic and fiscal considerations, nationalist passions were awakened by the possible danger that thousands of Polish railway employees would lose their positions and be replaced by Russians. The bill was supported not only by the right wing and center of the Duma but also by the Progressives and Kadets. Only the Poles and the left wing opposed it. On December 9, 1911, Żukowski, the Koło's economic expert and a representative of mining interests in Poland, declared that the money could be better spent on the construction of new railways. Of the nineteen official railway regions of Russia, Poland was only ninth in terms of mileage.[106] He spoke of the inefficiency of the state-owned railroads by comparison with the privately owned Warsaw-Vienna line. He also warned that the line would not be profitable to the state, and he expressed fears about the fate of the more than sixty-five thousand railroad employees whose economic situation

[105] *GDSO. 1911–1912 gg. Sessiia* V, III, 1240–41, 1252–62, 1271–74, 1262–68; *Sessia* V, IV, 1907–10.

[106] In fact, while the population of Poland was 7.6 percent of that of the Russian Empire, the railways in Poland amounted to 4.91 percent of those of the Empire. Siemieński, *La Pologne*, p. 622.

would worsen if they became state employees and whose very jobs would be endangered because they were Poles.[107]

Żukowski was answered by Prime Minister V. N. Kokovtsov, who defended the bill in person. He argued the legality of the action, described the bill as "a purely financial and economic question," and insisted that the state would make a profit from the railway. He stated that it was not a characteristic of the treasury "necessarily to desire to get rid of some in order to put others in their place." If the railroad employees working on the line were conscientious and wished to continue in their employment, "there is no reason to presume that they will be replaced and, furthermore, by a worse element." On the other hand, should "normal losses" or other circumstances necessitate the replacement of some workers by others, "then I do not know on what grounds the members of the State Duma who have spoken before me consider that Russians will necessarily be worse than those Poles who have worked on this line up to now." Kokovtsov referred to the two railway lines of Ivangorod-Dąbrowa and Warsaw-Terespol that had been acquired by the state in 1897 and 1900. He stated that Russians numbered no more than 28 percent of their employees. "Let honest workers from the local population . . . not worry about their fate, and they will work in confidence for the state."

Grabski replied that even a turnover of 28 percent represented a huge change of employees, while I. P. Pokrovskii, the Social Democrat, brushed aside the claim that the issue was financial and insisted that it was one of "militant nationalism."[108] The bill was rushed through the Duma without second and third readings, and an interpellation by Żukowski on April 24, 1912, concerning the replacement of

[107] *GDSO. 1911–1912 gg. Sessiia* V, I, 3547.
[108] *Ibid.*, pp. 3567–78, 3582–86.

Poles by Russians on the railway had no effect except to inflame the anger of the right. When Żukowski cited two excerpts from the reactionary newspaper *Grazhdanin* reporting that the minister of communications had presented to the Nationalists a list of individuals to be given positions on the Warsaw-Vienna line and that the list had been approved, the Nationalists indignantly denied the allegation. At the same time, Purishkevich demanded that the "hegemony" of the Poles in the Russian railways be liquidated.[109]

In sum, a large variety of relatively secondary legislation dealing with issues indirectly or directly affecting Russia's Poles revealed the almost insuperable difficulties encountered by the Koło in extracting even minimal concessions for Poland from the nationalistically inspired Third Duma. The sessions of this Duma also made manifest the political fragility of Octobrist support upon which the Koło had based its tactics. However, the legislative problems confronting the Koło were most graphically illustrated by the three principal issues affecting the Polish question in the years immediately preceding the outbreak of World War I: the western zemstvos, the separation of Chełm, and the problem of urban self-government in the Kingdom of Poland.

[109] *Ibid.*, III, 3112–18, 3123.

V

THE LAST TWO YEARS of Stolypin's tenure of office as prime minister witnessed an intensification of the nationalist course in both the government and the State Duma. As Stolypin's position in office weakened after the ministerial crisis of 1909, and as he relied on the support of the new Russian National party, his program increasingly emphasized nationalist themes. With regard to the Polish question, the greater emphasis was illustrated by the government's proposal to introduce zemstvo institutions in Russia's western provinces. The scheme was particularly important to Stolypin who, as marshal of the nobility in the province of Kovno and as governor of the province of Grodno, had acquired a full and personal awareness of the superior social and economic position of the Polish landowners over the Lithuanian and Belorussian peasantry.[1] He indicated more than once that, after the peasant land reform and an investigation of the general provincial administration, he

---

[1] Nicolas Savickij, "P. A. Stolypin," *Le Monde slave*, 4 (Nov. 1933), 227–28; M. P. Bok, *Vospominaniia o moem ottse P. A. Stolypine* (New York, 1953), p. 323.

82

attributed to this zemstvo bill a supreme importance.[2] Furthermore, the encouragement of Russian nationalism in the western borderland could be regarded as complementing Stolypin's agrarian reform by converting the peasantry into an anti-revolutionary and conservative force. In addition, in the Third Duma, the Russian National party had its main electoral stronghold in Belorussia, Bessarabia, and the right-bank Ukraine.[3]

The government's bill for the introduction of zemstvo institutions into six western provinces was deliberated and accepted by the Duma in May 1910, at the same time as the bill curtailing the authority of the Finnish parliament in matters of supposedly "imperial significance." The question of the western zemstvos had a long history. It first arose in connection with the introduction of zemstvos into the central provinces of Russia in 1864, but the proposal to extend these institutions to the western border provinces was rejected as untimely owing to the recent Polish insurrection of 1863. As a matter of fact, it was the deliberate policy of the government at the time to confine the zemstvo system to the strictly Russian areas of the Empire, the thirty-four central provinces, and to exclude it from the borderlands either where there were few noble landowners or where the upper classes were predominantly or heavily non-Russian as was the case with the Germans in the Baltic area and the Poles in the western provinces. In 1899 the question of zemstvos in the western provinces was raised again by I. L. Goremykin, then minister of the interior, but was disapproved on the insistence of Witte, who took the occasion to compose his celebrated memorandum on the incompati-

---

[2] V. N. Kokovtsov, *Iz moego proshlago: Vospominaniia 1903–1919* (Paris, 1933), I, 450–51.

[3] C. Jay Smith, "The Russian Third State Duma: An Analytical Profile," *Russian Review*, 17 (July 1958), 207.

bility of local self-government with the autocracy. Under D. S. Sipiagin, the matter was posed in the form of the creation of institutions of a purely administrative type. The law of April 2, 1903, was applied to the three Belorussian provinces of Vitebsk, Minsk, and Mogilev and, in 1904, to the three southwestern provinces of Kiev, Podolia, and Volhynia. However, this law, which established zemstvos ("margarine zemstvos") on the basis not of election but solely of administrative appointment, and then only on the provincial level, proved to be disappointing.

In 1906, during elections to the Second Duma, Stolypin proposed to the Council of Ministers the idea of introducing elective zemstvos by means of Article 87. Proportional elections would stabilize the numbers of Poles and Russians on zemstvo boards. This proposal aroused disapproval among Polish landowners, and the suggestion was postponed in order not to force the landowners into opposition to the government during a period of social disturbance. In May 1908, the Duma accepted a formula of the Octobrists and Moderate Rightists proposing to the government that it consider the establishment of zemstvos in the nine western provinces.[4]

However, the first action came from an unlikely source. On May 8, 1909, thirty-three rightists in the State Council led by D. I. Pikhno, the reactionary editor of the newspaper *Kievlanin*, introduced a proposal to alter the electoral law for elections to the upper house from nine western provinces: the six Belorussian and Little Russian provinces and also the three Lithuanian provinces of Vilno, Grodno, and Kovno. The proposal was motivated by the desire to reduce

[4] A. Ia. Avrekh, "Vopros o zapadnom zemstve i bankrotstvo Stolypina," *Istoricheskie zapiski*, 70 (1961), 65; Wierzchowski, *Sprawy Polski*, pp. 144–45; *GDSO. 1909–1910 gg. Sessiia III*, IV, pp. 729–34.

the number of Poles seated in the State Council. By the existing law, the elections in the non-zemstvo provinces of members to the State Council, one member for each province, were to take place in provincial assemblies of landowners who met high property qualifications. Since the large landlords in the nine western provinces were predominantly Poles, all nine of the elected members of the State Council from the western borderland were Poles. Accordingly, the thirty-three rightists proposed that the nine provinces be grouped into the three electoral districts of Vilno, Mogilev, and Kiev and that within each district there should be two electoral conferences instead of one: one conference for the Polish landholders and one for the non-Polish. Furthermore, each electoral district was to elect two Russian members to the State Council and one Polish member, a total of six Russians and three Poles.[5]

Ignoring the fact that all nine Poles in the State Council belonged to the center group upon which the government relied, Stolypin reacted favorably and rapidly to the rightist initiative. "The basic thought . . . is in general recognized by the government as acceptable."[6] On May 12, 1909, the Ministry of the Interior introduced a "most urgent" proposal in the Duma that elections to the State Council from the western provinces be postponed for one year. Since the spring session of the Duma was drawing to a close and an important bill could not be considered before the autumn, and since elections to the State Council from the western provinces were scheduled for the summer, there was the danger of a repetition of the results of past elections. Consequently, the government's proposal was a hasty expedient preliminary to more fundamental legislation. It was de-

[5] *GSSO. 1908–1909 gg. Sessiia IV* (St. Petersburg, 1909), pp. 1933–50.
[6] *Ibid.*, p. 1941.

fended by Stolypin with characteristic force and authority: "The government is guided by the realization of the need to listen to the just demands of the native Russian population of the borderlands . . . and to support them with all the strength of governmental authority."[7] The proposal was passed by the Duma on May 30, although in a slightly altered form. The term of office of members of the State Council was not actually extended, but the summer elections were to be for a term of only one year.[8] The measure was accepted by the State Council on June 8 and became law in July.[9]

On January 20, 1910, the western zemstvo bill was introduced in the Duma by the government with the special provision, in the nature of an admonition, that the bill must enter into force as a law by July 1, 1910.[10] However, the bill did not propose a simple extension to the western provinces of the zemstvo law of 1890 that obtained for the central provinces of Russia. The law of 1890 was based on social class and property qualifications, and its application in the borderland would have had the same consequence as in the interior, namely, landlord dominance over the peasantry. But the large landlords in the west were Poles. Russian land ownership in the region had been fostered and encouraged by the government after 1863, but large-scale Russian landholdings did not compare with the Polish, and the Russian proprietors were for the most part absentee. Also, many of the Belorussian and Ukrainian peasantry, officially considered to be Russian, were Catholic and economically dependent upon Polish landlords. By contrast, there was a significant stratum of nationally conscious in-

[7] *GDSO. 1908–1909 gg. Sessiia II*, IV, 2756.
[8] *Ibid.*, p. 2831.
[9] *GSSO. 1908–1909 gg. Sessiia IV*, p. 2363.
[10] *Gosudarstvennaia Duma. Obzor deiatel'nosti gosudarstvennoi Dumy tret'iago sozyva*, II, 81.

dependent Russian peasant proprietors, especially in the southwestern provinces.[11]

These factors were reflected in the zemstvo bill. First, no zemstvos were to be introduced into the three northwestern provinces of Vilno, Kovno, and Grodno. In the first two, the property of Russian landlords was too insignificant in area. Grodno was dropped for the sake of the administrative unity of the governor generalship of "the northwestern region" and because many Belorussian Catholics were under Polish influence. In the remaining six provinces, the original problem of securing the election of Russians to the State Council was subordinated to the task of making the new zemstvos an effective instrument of Russian nationalism. To this end, various modifications were made in the zemstvo law of 1890. Elections by social class were eliminated and national chambers were introduced for zemstvo elections on both the provincial and district (*uezd*) levels. The number of members of Polish and Russian nationality was artificially established. The percentage of a given nationality's population within a province was added to the percentage of zemstvo taxes to which the land and immovable property of the nationality within a district were subject, and the result was divided in half. The final figure determined the percentage of zemstvo voters of a given nationality. For instance, if Poles constituted 2 percent of the population and paid 38 percent of the taxes, they would have 20 percent of the votes. However, since the unconditional application of this percentage rule to the Russian chamber would have effected a peasant majority in the zemstvos, peasant representation was radically curtailed by another rule. In district zemstvos, peasant members elected by communes might not exceed one-third of the

[11] A. Ia. Avrekh, *Tsarizm i tret'eiiun'skaia sistema* (Moscow, 1966), pp. 93–94.

total membership, no matter what the number of the peasant population or the extent of peasant landholdings. Furthermore, there was to be no communal peasant representation in the provincial zemstvos.

The government bill also provided that the Orthodox clergy of the six western provinces should send three representatives to each district zemstvo and four to each provincial one. This provision differed from the law of 1890, which allowed only a single church delegate to each district and provincial zemstvo. The bill likewise stipulated that the chairman of every zemstvo executive board and no fewer than one-half of the members of the executive board, as well as half of the zemstvo employees, must be of Russian nationality. Finally, a separate article specifically excluded Jews from zemstvo elections, a reaffirmation of the law of 1890.[12]

On January 25, the Duma referred the bill to the committee on local self-government. The committee was dominated by the Octobrists, who recommended slight alterations designed to liberalize certain, but not all, features of the government project and to modify its nationalistic bias. The committee suggested that instead of the two voting standards of population and property to determine the number of voters in each national category, there should be a single standard, that of property. This alteration was in line with the current principle that only those who fulfilled a certain property requirement and paid zemstvo taxes were entitled to participate in zemstvo affairs. It also signified a slight increase in the Polish vote. In addition, the committee recommended that the determination of property ownership by nationality should be made on a provincial but not on a district basis, since the concentra-

[12] *Gosudarstvennaia Duma. Prilozheniia k stenograficheskim otchetam. 1909–1910 gg.*, II, No. 330, pp. 29–62.

tion of land in Polish hands in certain districts would give a majority of the zemstvo seats to the Poles there. On a provincial basis of property assessment, the Polish share would fluctuate between a minimum of 13 percent and a maximum of 27 percent.

The committee further recommended that the land and immovable property requirement for participation in zem-stvo elections be reduced by half. It also proposed the principle of "facultativeness," namely, that on the district level, but not on the provincial one, the two national chambers might meet as a single electoral assembly when this was so desired by a qualified majority of two-thirds of each chamber. This principle would have allowed some contact between Poles and peasants at the strictly local level. With regard to the government proposal concerning representation of the Orthodox clergy in the zemstvos, the only committee change was that the number of priests in the provincial zemstvo be the same as that for the district zemstvo, that is, three instead of the original four. The committee also advocated the formation in each district not of one electoral conference (*sezd*) but of two conferences that would be preliminary to the zemstvo electoral assembly (*sobranie*) and would divide the voters into two categories: those owning property from one-fifth to the full requirement and those owning from one-tenth to one-fifth of the requirement. This alteration averted the possibility that moderate landowners in a single electoral conference would be engulfed by the more numerous small landowners. Finally, the committee rejected the government's demand for a guaranteed majority of Russians on the executive boards of the zemstvos and among zemstvo employees, since the Russian element in any event would be "the master of the situation" owing to its majority in the zemstvo assemblies.[13]

[13] *Ibid.*, pp. 2–11.

The tone of the debate in the Duma on the zemstvo bill was set by Stolypin's address on May 8. Displaying a paternalistic but apprehensive nationalism, he insisted on the need "to create a new electoral assembly in which the rights of the economically weak Russian majority would be protected from economically and culturally strong Polish interference." The government, Stolypin conceded, agreed on the value of utilizing all the local elements in the western territory, but—and this was the burden of his argument— "only to the extent that this does not contradict the predominantly national concerns pursued by the government in the western area . . . the necessity of subordinating the zemstvo idea to that of the state." In his emphasis on the weakness of the Russian element by comparison with the long and deeply entrenched Polish one, the prime minister posed, and rejected, the question whether "now that the time has come for greater freedom and independence for local groups . . . the government is justified in leaving the Russian forces to themselves . . . in renouncing assistance to those weak offshoots of the Russian state which have not yet grown strong there and which cannot yet defend themselves alone." If a minimal participation of the Russian element in the zemstvo had to be ruled out because of the absence of that element, then, Stolypin asserted, it would be preferable not to introduce the institution. He gave this as his reason for deferring the introduction of zemstvos into the three northwestern provinces of Vilno, Kovno, and Grodno. Referring to the Polish uprisings of 1830 and 1863, he observed: "These are the historical lessons which demonstrate, I think, clearly enough that a state like Russia cannot and should not renounce with impunity carrying out its historical tasks." Stolypin concluded his general observations with a broad defense of the idea of national chambers.

The entire historical past of the western area speaks for
the necessity of protecting it from a national struggle at the
time of zemstvo elections, of protecting it from the dominating influence of the Polish element in its economic
life . . . . Yes, it is necessary to introduce the zemstvo . . .
but historical causes oblige placing state limitations for
the defense of the Russian element which otherwise will
unavoidably be squeezed and pushed out. From all of this
there follows for me the need for national chambers.[14]

Stolypin's detailed replies to the recommendations of the
Duma's committee on local self-government emphasized
the degree of his attachment to the zemstvo bill, the significance which he ascribed to it, and his obdurate opposition
to any weakening of its anti-Polish character. The chords
most often struck were fear of Polish assertiveness, anxiety
about the lack of local Russian initiative, and insistence
upon guidance and direction by the central government.
Stolypin dismissed the committee's suggestion on facultativeness as inadmissible. The chambers had to be exclusively electoral; they should not be convertible into
political assemblies that would inflame national passions
by attempting to conduct joint electoral campaigns. The
Poles, with their discipline, culture, and strength, would
be able to secure the election of the Russians they desired
either through a majority of the electors or through Russian
absenteeism. Even the establishment of national chambers
would not in itself guarantee and protect Russian state
interests. The preponderance of these interests over all
others could be realized only through the predominance of
the Russian element within the zemstvo assemblies.

Stolypin pointed to the inadequacy of the principle of
zemstvo representation on the basis of property alone as

[14] *GDSO. 1909–1910 gg. Sessiia III*, IV, 774–87.

recommended by the Duma committee. The committee had noted the unfavorable position of Russians in several districts with respect to land ownership, but the committee's corrective was "much more dangerous," namely, the determination of the number of Polish district zemstvo members on the basis of the total amount of property owned in the province. This unhappy corrective would give the Poles representation in purely Russian districts, and in all six of the western provinces "the general number of Polish members would be of a dangerous proportion from the viewpoint of Russian interests." The number would admittedly nowhere exceed 30 percent, but "the peasants and small landholders . . . are under the strong economic pressure of the Polish landlords. The Russian element, the Russian landlords, are not united and, unfortunately, often do not live in the region." Stolypin also urged retention of the original government proposal for representation of the Orthodox clergy in the district and provincial zemstvos and referred to the "beneficent influence" of the Church on the peasantry.

The prime minister took exception to the proposition of the Duma committee that once the Russian element had a majority in the zemstvo assemblies its position in the organization of the zemstvo would be secured by that fact alone. "Only through the force of a firm law can a minimum of the Russian element [that is, more than 50 percent] be secured in these institutions . . . a number which the Polish element could never count upon in terms of population percentages." In addition, a "firm" law was also imperative with regard to the nationality of zemstvo employees because of the ease and cheapness in hiring Poles, the possible grant of personal favors, and "a certain good-heartedness and compliancy on the part of the Russian element." Stolypin's address ended on a resounding key: "The bill . . . puts a limit to further secular, national, political conflict . . . by solidly defending . . . Russian state principles. The confirmation in the Duma of these principles . . . will forestall many misunderstandings and dissatisfactions by affirming openly and without hypocrisy that the western region is and forever will be Russian."[15]

Stolypin defended his bill before the Duma on one more occasion. He conceded that the government was prepared to accept the committee recommendation that the property requirement be reduced by half. However, he pointed out that, besides the peasant representation of one-third in the district zemstvos, peasants as delegates of individual small landholders would have increased access to zemstvo assemblies under the smaller property requirement. "Therefore, the increase of the number of peasants is possible . . . only at the expense of the cultured elements of the region." Stolypin's conciliatory social concession was accompanied by a fresh outburst of nationalist polemic when he again defended the double electoral percentage standard of nationality and property. The Poles constituted only 4 percent of the population and, furthermore, their property had been acquired not naturally and legally,

> but by virtue of an historical squall that swept over this area and overthrew everything Russian. It is impossible to take an exceptional and anti-national historical phenomenon—one unfavorable to the Russians besides—as the basis, the sole basis, of the entire bill. It is impossible to dismiss the whole past with a wave of the hand . . . . If you regard the principles stated by me as being incorrect or odious, then the government takes this odium upon itself.[16]

Stimulated by Stolypin's animated presentation, the Rightists gave vent to violent diatribes against the Poles as

[15] *Ibid.*, pp. 787–91.
[16] *Ibid.*, pp. 1391–92.

a gangrene in the body of Russia. They characterized the western zemstvos as a bulwark against the spread of Polish influence in the country and their establishment as a "preventive war" with the Polish nation designed to destroy its striving for national independence. Bishop Eulogius stated that the question was clearly whether the western provinces were to be Russian or whether they were to be considered "lost lands" that the Poles might reclaim. The Rightists also demanded the restoration of the provision dealing with the representation of the Orthodox clergy on the zemstvos. Speaking for the Nationalists, S. M. Bogdanov stated that his party would not support the committee version, except for the reduction of the property requirement by half, as a "democratization"[17] of the measure.

Although a majority of the Octobrists voted for the committee version of the zemstvo bill, the party came close to being split down the middle. It was revealed that at a party conference on May 11, after a dispute about whether the committee recommendation of the single voting standard of property should be supported against the government's proposal of the two standards of property and population, twenty-five voted for the committee and nineteen for the government. As a result, it was decided that each deputy should vote as he wished on each article of the bill. Since all parties to the left of the Octobrists voted against the bill, the Duma found itself split into two almost equal halves.[18] With the Octobrists themselves divided into a right and a left wing, the large center of the Third Duma was threatened by the issue of nationalism. In speeches supporting the single voting standard that would increase slightly the number of Polish zemstvo electors, three Oc-

[17] *Ibid.*, pp. 890–910, 919–26, 947–60, 792–96.
[18] *Novoe vremia*, May 12, 1910; May 14, 1910.

tobrist deputies, I. N. Glebov, M. A. Iskritskii, and A. E. Favorskii, addressed themselves to the parties to the right with the assurance that this increase would not seriously influence the composition of the zemstvos.[19]

The moderate statements of the Polish Koło resembled those that had been made during the Opole interpellation. It was argued that the Polish landowners in the western provinces were loyal subjects and natives of the area. They were closely involved with local issues and the economy, whereas the more recently imported Russian gentry were mostly absentee and indifferent to the life of the provinces. Consequently, the zemstvo institutions foreseen by the government would simply be a bureaucratic machine designed to play upon and intensify national friction. Grabski denied that the Poles were using their position to harm the state and charged that accusations of Polish "aggressiveness" were simply a "strained interpretation." Stanisław Wańkowicz asserted that the government wished to replace the "margarine zemstvo" with a "masquerade zemstvo." Like his colleagues, he emphasized the loyalty of the Poles to the state. "We Poles have already declared from this tribune, and are now declaring, that we stand and shall permanently stand for the point of view of the state and you cannot reproach us with one act against the state . . . . We Poles are by conviction monarchists and constitutionalists. You will always find in us advocates of justice and legality, and you know this." He stated that the Poles had placed a "cross" on their past as a state, on a "grave," and that "we go to this grave only in order to draw lessons on how not to act."[20]

The principal critics and opponents of the bill were the

[19] *GDSO. 1909–1910 gg. Sessiia III,* IV, 858–69, 937–38.
[20] *Ibid.,* pp. 1215, 1120–31.

Kadets. Their opposition was based on the thesis that the government's nationality policy was not only not averting a new revolution but actually precipitating one. Although, at a party conference, some Kadets advocated acceptance of the bill with "the necessary corrections," and Miliukov explained that national chambers were not "contrary to the program of the party," it was nevertheless decided to vote against the bill.[21] F. A. Golovin, a moderate and respected figure and the former president of the Second Duma, delivered an attack of unusual sharpness upon the government. He declared that the purpose of the bill was to deflect public attention from the most serious internal issues by assailing the Poles. By arousing nationalist emotions, the government expected to rule by dividing society into mutually hostile sections. But such a policy would not succeed in the long run and the danger of a new revolution would mount, while the exclusion of the Poles as the most advanced element in the western provinces from participation in zemstvo activities would degrade the institution. Rodichev, considered best disposed toward the Poles, warned that a state where civil rights were arbitrarily determined by administrative authorities could not survive. A. I. Shingarev cautioned that the government's nationality policy was the same that in the past "had led to Sevastopol, Tsushima, and Mukden." The Progressive V. S. Sokolov admonished that official antipathy toward non-Russian nationalities in the borderlands might cause them to side with Russia's enemies in the event of an international conflict. The Kadet historian I. V. Luchitskii created a tumult on the right side of the chamber by asserting that the government's claim to be defending "the Russian people" in the western provinces was hollow since the Eastern Slavs

[21] Avrekh, "Vopros o zapadnom zemstve," p. 81; Wierzchowski, *Sprawy Polski*, p. 151.

there "were completely separate with their own national physiognomy."[22]

The Labor Group made a special declaration in opposition to the bill, demanding a genuinely democratic zemstvo structure throughout the country without any limitations on the basis of property or nationality. They also condemned the bill for subordinating the zemstvo to the bureaucracy and for sacrificing the peasantry to the interests of a small group of Russian landowners. Conservative peasant deputies from the western provinces took an active part in the debates and, although their addresses were suffused with rabidly anti-Polish observations, they expressed dissatisfaction over the limitations on the numbers of peasant electors for the zemstvos and the disproportionate taxation between the property of peasants and landlords.

Pokrovskii, the Social Democratic orator, characterized the legislation regarding Finland and the western zemstvos as the beginning of a new era in the activity of the government and the Duma, with whose repressive nationalist spirit he contrasted the international and democratic one of his own party. He particularly challenged the discrimination against the local peasantry embodied in the bill and pointed out that, from the democratic point of view, the hostility between the Polish and the Russian landowners was a matter of indifference since both were anxious to maintain their economic hegemony over the peasants. "On the one hand, the Polish landowners are allowed to participate in the zemstvo because they are landowners but, on the other hand, their rights are limited because of nationalistic hatred and rivalry. . . . There is no conflict between the Polish and Russian landowners, merely unfair competition."[23]

The zemstvo bill was finally passed by the Duma on

[22] *GDSO. 1909–1910 gg. Sessiia III*, IV, 804–10, 1109, 994, 836, 1034.
[23] *Ibid.*, pp. 1229, 1021, 1092–1106.

97

May 29, 1910, by a vote of 165 to 139. Its principal sup-
porters were the Nationalists and the right wing of the
Octobrists. Only a few changes were made in the government's bill and the moderate Octobrists, who advocated the
committee recommendations on facultativeness and the
single electoral requirement of property, were defeated. In
the final version, the Duma rejected the articles on the obligatory representation of the Orthodox clergy and on the
Russian nationality of the chairmen of the zemstvo executive boards and the majority of zemstvo employees. However, the Duma accepted the provision that a majority of
the members of executive boards must be of Russian nationality. The Duma bill also included the property requirement reduced by half and the principle of the two
preliminary electoral conferences. It was also established
that each district should delegate one peasant to the provincial zemstvo.[24]

It was the fate of the zemstvo bill in the State Council
that brought about the ministerial and parliamentary crisis
of March 1911. This crisis proved to be a Pyrrhic victory
for Stolypin and ended in the collapse of his political career. The government's project was unexpectedly defeated
by the narrow and conservative State Council, which, furthermore, was influenced by the personal intrigues of reac-
tionaries against the prime minister. The negative vote
inflamed the impetuous and headstrong Stolypin. He suddenly submitted his resignation and forced the emperor to
enact the zemstvo bill under Article 87 of the Fundamental
Laws.

Although the leadership of the opposition to Stolypin's
bill was furnished by the right wing of the State Council,
which constituted the rampart of reaction, the principal
voting group in the Council was that of the center. It was

[24] *Ibid.*, p. 2839.

the center that expressed most dissatisfaction with the non-class formula of the zemstvo bill, the lowered property requirement, and the principle of national chambers.[25] According to the shrewd but prejudiced and isolated Witte, who was then a member of the State Council:

> The moderate nobility were against this project because they found it impossible to draw a distinction between the Polish nobility and the Russian nobility. They pointed out, not without reason, that distinctive national chambers for the selection of Russian and Polish nobles would result not in the union of the nobility in these provinces but in their complete disunion, whereas at the time there existed a complete solidarity between Russian and Polish nobles in the vast majority of instances.[26]

In addition, the conservatives of the State Council feared that the bill gave too broad a representation in the western zemstvos to the peasantry. They rejected what they regarded as Stolypin's demagogic maneuver, since they feared that the peasants in the western provinces would swamp the landlords and also that there would be pressure to introduce such a system of zemstvo elections into central Russia. Indeed, the opposition of the State Council to the extension of zemstvo institutions within the Empire was sustained after Stolypin. In 1912, bills passed by the Duma for the creation of zemstvos in Siberia and the Don region were vetoed by the Council; in 1913, a bill to establish zemstvos in the province of Archangel was rejected. Although, in the same year, zemstvos were introduced in the provinces of Stavropol, Orenburg, and Astrakhan, on the insistence of the State Council the native Turko-Tartar inhabitants as well as the Cossack settlements were

172305

[25] A. S. Izgoev, "Politicheskaia zhizn' v Rossii," *Russkaia mysl'* (April 1911), pp. 3–4.
[26] Witte, *Vospominaniia*, p. 542.

excluded and the property requirement was actually doubled.[27]

The State Council had formed a special committee as early as May 5, 1910, to examine the zemstvo bill, but on November 3 Prince E. N. Trubetskoi, the chairman, commented on new developments in the Duma, namely, the decision to reduce by half the property requirement for participation in zemstvo elections. In his opinion, a situation would thereby be created in the six western provinces "such as is not to be encountered elsewhere, not in a single zemstvo province of Russia."[28] The protracted deliberations of the special committee effectively postponed discussion of the bill in the State Council until the end of January 1911. Stolypin, however, who was aware of the opposition of the rightist members of the committee, did not attribute great significance to any obstacles or to the loud disagreement evoked by the problem of national chambers. In fact, the bill was supported only by a small group in the center, "the party of the brothers-in-law," led by A. B. Neidhardt, who was married to the prime minister's sister.

In the debates, which began at the end of January, criticism of the bill was directed essentially against the introduction of national chambers and, to a lesser degree, the reduction of the property qualification. The main argument against the chambers was that they introduced an anti-state principle that threatened the unity of the Empire. Witte's view was that national chambers "could not be tolerated so long as there is preserved in Russia a clear and firm awareness of the integrity of the Russian state principle." Their introduction would be tantamount to the admission that the non-Russian inhabitants of the Empire

---

[27] Vladimir Trutovskii, *Sovremennoe zemstvo* (Petrograd, 1914) pp. 178–79, 211.

[28] *GSSO. 1910–1911 gg. Sessiia VI* (St. Petersburg, 1911), p. 155.

might have interests different from the interests of the state. A. D. Obolenskii, a representative of the center, circulated among the members of the State Council a special memorandum demonstrating that zemstvos could be introduced in the western provinces without the national chambers, which "exist nowhere in a single social or state institution in Russia" and actually represented a political danger. "If we allow this principle in the western region, why not permit it in other localities of Russia?" Unfavorable comparisons were made with Austria, which had introduced universal suffrage in 1907, by the rightist N. P. Balashov and by Prince E. N. Trubetskoi of the center. Even the liberal M. M. Kovalevskii expressed the opinion that the national chambers would inaugurate a movement which "I might characterize as renunciation of the all-state idea in favor of recognition of the demands of the nationalities."

The Polish spokesman, Aleksander Meysztowicz, referring to Poles in both the Duma and the State Council who defended the interests of all the landed proprietors of the Empire, both Polish and Russian, sounded the class theme when he observed: "After the sad experience of the recent past, it would seem to follow that people should be divided not according to nationalities but into the adherents and the enemies of social order and the social system. However, the bill divides Russian and Polish conservatives into national chambers and so strengthens disunion." He was seconded by the rightist N. A. Zinoviev, who stated: "The Poles say that they adhere to their nationality, but not in those instances when it is a question of the Russian state; that, in the interests of the Russian state, they are in complete solidarity with us. I think that this can be believed."[29]

The burden of the opposition to the reduction of the property requirement, in the light of the nonclass character

[29] *Ibid.*, pp. 814–18, 923, 1224, 909, 949.

of the prospective western zemstvo, was that the effect would be the democratization of the zemstvo and that this, in turn, would have harmful political consequences. One of the most fervent adversaries of the bill on this ground, apart from the Polish circle, was Zinoviev. He argued that the reduction would inflame the lower classes against the upper and provide a precedent for the rest of the country. He also raised the specter of Ukrainian nationalism. The hostility within the State Council to the reduced property requirement reflected the continuing conservative and reactionary resistance to Stolypin's agrarian program with its supposed "demagogy." The protests against the democratization of the zemstvo did not actually refer to the intended total of one-third of the zemstvo members from the communal peasantry, but to the increased representation of independent peasant proprietors in the villages of the western provinces. The peasants had the right of legal participation in elections to the zemstvo and to the Duma, not only as the representatives of the commune but also as individual landowners, provided that the property they purchased or acquired was no less than one-tenth of the complete property requirement. The one-third peasant representation in the zemstvo foreseen by the bill belonged to the former category. The peasants in the second category, as the proprietors of a portion of the full property requirement, were to participate in district zemstvo elections as individuals in a conference of small landholders that would send one delegate for each full requirement to the electoral assembly. The assembly, in turn, would select the allotted number of district zemstvo members.

The criticism of the State Council was directed against the extension of this second category of peasant electors. No protests were raised against the one-third limit of peasant zemstvo members chosen by the village communes.

Indeed, some demands were made for an increase in the number of members from peasant communes, an actual extension of the one-third limit imposed by the government's bill. Witte spoke out against the reduction of the property requirement and maintained that the principal bulwark of the zemstvos in the western provinces would be the "Orthodox peasantry," whom he opposed to the second category of individual peasant proprietors that would be introduced through the lowered requirement. The Poles also advocated retention of the full property requirement and an increase in communal peasant representation. M. M. Kovalevskii likewise attacked the one-third limitation.[30]

Moreover, the State Council remained unmoved by a concession made by Stolypin whereby the one-half property requirement would be kept but the right to participate in electoral assemblies would be accorded only to owners of no less than one-fifth of the requirement. This provision would prevent an influx of very small landowners through the electoral conferences. Since the requirement in the bill accepted by the Duma fluctuated for the six provinces from 100 *desiatiny* in Kiev and Volhynia to 600 *desiatiny* in Minsk, the minimal ownership of land that would guarantee eligibility to participate in zemstvo elections would vary between 20 and 120 *desiatiny*, that is, the holdings of a fairly prosperous peasant proprietor. Consequently, the majority of the State Council were opposed to, or at least suspicious of, that element which was the object of Stolypin's "wager on the strong." They may have feared that even the wealthiest element in the village would not be secure as a counterrevolutionary force. Furthermore, because of the relative weakness of the Russian landlords in the western provinces, the State Council was afraid that the wealthy peasants might acquire a strong position and com-

[30] *Ibid.*, pp. 1308, 954, 1316, 846, 816, 1258, 1308, 1360.

pete with the nobility in zemstvo institutions. Finally, the State Council was alive to the danger of a precedent that might betoken the future extension of this more broadly based zemstvo principle to the central provinces of Russia. Even the conservative *Novoe vremia* observed: "An outlived class concept is attempting to buy itself a return to the past."[31]

Prime Minister Stolypin addressed the State Council on three occasions in forceful defense of the zemstvo bill. On January 28, the first day of general debate, he immediately agreed that the right to participate in electoral conferences should be confined to owners of not less than one-fifth of the property requirement. On the other hand, the government would be obliged "to insist" on the introduction of three and four clergymen into the district and provincial zemstvos, the selection of chairmen of zemstvo boards from persons of Russian nationality, and the establishment of national chambers, "without which the bill, in the opinion of the government, would hardly bring the expected benefit. Therefore, the government . . . considers as unacceptable any alteration of this part of the bill."[32]

Stolypin's first speech made explicit the demands of the government. His addresses on February 1 and March 4 sounded the loud trumpet call of his narrow Russian nationalism. In the first speech, he began by refuting the possible Russian charge that the law of 1903 was adequate and the actual Polish charge that the western zemstvo question had arisen by chance as a result of the decision to alter the electoral procedure for membership in the State Council from the western provinces and to oppress the Poles in a new area, that of self-government. "The question of introducing zemstvos concerned the present government as

[31] March 8, 1911.
[32] *GSSO. 1910–1911 gg. Sessiia VI*, pp. 790–91.

early as 1906." Action was merely delayed by the Duma's hostility to the extension of the zemstvo act of 1890 to the western provinces, by the need to guarantee Russian interests, and—"one must be open about it"—by the special cohesiveness of the Poles in the first two Dumas. The Russian defenders of the act of 1903 might emphasize the fact that the Russian element did not play an active enough role in local life. "This argument, of course, is correct but not the conclusions drawn from it." Stolypin then dealt with the contention that he was proposing a zemstvo in name only which might serve as soil for the development not of economic independence but rather of national strife. He countered that a political approach was unfortunately necessitated by the favored position of the Poles.

> What is termed the introduction of the zemstvo into politics is really a precautionary inoculation; an insurance against politics, against the predominance of one part of the population, one element, over others, a predominance which, without equalization by the regulators that are not in vain in the hands of the state, will give a one-sided cast to the zemstvo institutions and, through them, to the entire region .... It is the introduction of general zemstvo organizations into the region without any alterations that would bring a feverish political conflict into its life.

In answer to the argument that there would not be enough non-Poles to create permanent zemstvo organizations, Stolypin referred to the government's acceptance of the Duma's improvement of the bill which halved the property requirement. "The composition of those who meet the one-half property requirement is qualitatively adequate with regard to education . . . and there will be an insignificant number of illiterates." Furthermore, the reduced requirement would have the effect of bringing about a certain cohesion among the moderate but educated Russian landholders who might otherwise be engulfed in a sea of small electors. "My personal opinion is that people of little property and education will play a small role in the work of the zemstvo and that educated peasant landowners will participate well in zemstvo affairs."

Stolypin once more insisted on the role of the clergy in zemstvo assemblies "as a solder between the peasant delegates and the Russians who fulfill the property requirement." He also persisted in his demand that the chairmen of zemstvo executive boards be Russian. Asserting that the Poles, who numbered no more than 4 percent of the population, would receive representation of up to 16 percent, he concluded his speech on a strident note by explaining why Poles and Russians could not elect each other in common but had to be divided into separate electoral bodies. The reason was simply that the Poles would favor only Russians who were openly Polonophile. "Why do the Poles in every assembly, in every institution, group themselves by nationality? . . . Because they belong to a nation welded together by national grief, united by historical misfortune and by ancient and ambitious dreams; because they belong to a nation with a single policy—the homeland." The Russian population, by contrast, was ingenuous and politically inexperienced, composed of recent landholders who had acquired estates after the insurrection of 1863 and small proprietors of peasant origin.[33]

In his final speech before the State Council on March 4, Stolypin outlined the government's intention of "paralyzing" the predominant influence of the Poles in the western provinces, although he maintained that the Russian state was not opposed to everything Polish as such, but simply to an unchecked role of the Poles in the zemstvos.

[33] *Ibid.*, pp. 866–79.

It is obviously possible to act otherwise, but that would depend on a different understanding of the idea of the state. It is possible to understand the state as a combination of separate individuals, races, and nationalities held together by a single general law and administration. Such a state is an amalgam; it observes and protects existing relationships. But it is also possible to comprehend the state in a different fashion; it is possible to think of the state as a force, as a union in pursuit of national historical principles. Such a state, fulfilling a national legacy, has a will, has the power of coercion; such a state bends the rights of individuals and groups to the rights of the whole. I revere Russia as such a whole. I esteem Russian legislators as the preeminent bearers of such an idea of the state. Gentlemen, the decision is yours.

Stolypin concluded on an almost menacing note: "I must affirm one thing. The government considers the question of national divisions a question of state significance, the central issue of the present bill."[34]

This "central issue" was decided by the State Council on March 4 when the upper house rejected the provision on national chambers by a vote of 92 to 68.[35] The critical factor in the negative vote was the opposition of the right wing in the Council. Long before the consideration of the matter by the chamber, the leader of the rightist group, P. N. Durnovo, had handed the emperor a memorandum characterizing the separation of the Russian peasants in the western provinces into special electoral bodies as politically dangerous. Such a step would alienate from the government in that region the entire class of Polish landowners who were completely loyal to Russia. Furthermore, it might even strengthen anti-Russian tendencies among those who

[34] *Ibid.*, pp. 1240–41.
[35] *Ibid.*, p. 1256.

were pro-Austrian. The consequence of such an artificial measure would be that the educated landowning class would completely avoid local zemstvo work, which would fall into the hands of the peasantry and a few Russian officials. Before the discussion of the bill by the State Council, another rightist, V. F. Trepov, who was close to the emperor, obtained an audience with the ruler and persuaded him to allow the rightists to vote according to their conscience. Trepov met Baron V. B. Fredericks, the court minister, before the audience and heatedly informed him that the bill was a completely revolutionary invention which would alienate from the zemstvos all those people in the western provinces who were educated and conservative. Furthermore, he charged, it was all being done exclusively for the benefit of the petty Russian intelligentsia, which wanted to run everything.[36]

The upshot of the matter was that Stolypin tendered his resignation to the emperor on the day after the vote on the national chambers in the State Council. Despite his own role in the affair, Nicholas was taken aback. Using his sudden resignation as an ultimatum, Stolypin demanded the prorogation of both houses of the legislature, the enactment of the zemstvo bill as a temporary measure under Article 87 of the Fundamental Laws, and then its reintroduction into the Duma in the same form as that in which it had been originally passed by the lower house. Stolypin's parliamentary maneuver was essentially unconstitutional since Article 87 was merely intended to allow the emperor to issue emergency decrees whenever the legislature was actually in recess. Such decrees, furthermore, had to be ratified by the legislature within two months of its next meeting. The prime minister expected the rightists in the upper house to support the bill the second time, and he demanded

[36] Kokovtsov, *Iz moego proshlago*, pp. 452–53.

that Durnovo and Trepov be excluded from the State Council for the remainder of the year. After three days of vacillation, the unprepared emperor reluctantly yielded. On March 11, the Senate received an imperial order for the suspension of the State Duma and the State Council from March 12 to March 14 on the basis of Article 99 of the Fundamental Laws that allowed the emperor to prorogue the legislature. The Duma version of the zemstvo bill was promulgated in accordance with Article 87, and Durnovo and Trepov were sent on leave until January 1, 1912. Nevertheless, on the very day of the prorogation, the State Council succeeded in casting a final vote on the entire bill, which it rejected, 134 to 23.[37] Moreover, Stolypin had finally overplayed his hand, and the forcible tactics that had carried the day in 1906 proved to be unacceptable in 1911— unacceptable to the tsar, to the legislature, and to the public. Stolypin's personal influence and authority underwent an immediate eclipse and only his tragic death in September 1911 prevented his pending political disgrace.[38]

The passage of the zemstvo bill by the Duma illustrated once more the profound difficulties faced by the Poles in the legislature. General expressions of good will by the Duma center faded away when concrete issues arose in areas where nationalist feelings were strong. Specific concessions that were made to the Poles were invariably insignificant and marginal. The Octobrists' reform programs appeared to be losing ground to nationalistic tendencies. Furthermore, as in the case of the zemstvo bill, when the government took the initiative and gave a special impetus to the nationalist course, the conclusion was foregone and even vaguely liberal principles were disregarded. During

[37] *GSSO. 1910–1911 gg. Sessiia VI*, p. 1362.
[38] For details on these consequences of the zemstvo bill, see my article, "Stolypin's Last Crisis," *California Slavic Studies*, 3 (1964), 105ff.

the debates on the bill, the Octobrist I. S. Klimenko created a sensation when he commented on the absence of firm principles. He referred to the first proclamation of the Union of October 17 that had spoken of the broad development of local self-government throughout the Empire.

> The proposed bill is constructed on other bases, on the principle of national chambers, and, as such . . . contradicts the principles of the party to which I belong. . . . The attention of the entire country is directed towards the Duma center . . . and the country sees with sorrow that the center is not guided by firm principles. The Third Duma has existed for three years, and for three years we orthodox Octobrists have had to endure, to submit, and to compromise our principles.[39]

[39] *GDSO. 1909–1910 gg. Sessiia III*, IV, 1229–30.

VI

THE SEPARATION OF CHEŁM

THE DECISION to separate the area of Chełm from Poland in order to make a new Russian province of it was the crowning act of Stolypin's nationalist policy; that decision had a long history behind it. The area involved, a "Polish Alsace-Lorraine,"[1] lay on the left bank of the upper Bug River and comprised the eastern parts of the Polish provinces of Siedlce and Lublin. The northern region, in the province of Siedlce, was part of eastern Podlasie and was more solidly Polish than the southern part. The latter area, between the Bug and Wieprz rivers, contained a mixed Polish-Ukrainian population and had been colonized simultaneously from east and west. The intermingling of the Poles and Ukrainians had been facilitated by the Union of Brest in 1595–1596 and the establishment of the Uniate Church. Indeed, after the forcible reunion of the Uniates in western Russia with the official church in 1839, Chełm became the last remaining outpost of the Uniate Church in the Empire. However, in 1875, after the impetus given by the Polish rising of 1863, the Union of Brest was formally dissolved and the Uniates

---

[1] "The Country of Chełm," *Polish Encyclopedia* (Geneva, 1925), II, 728.

in the provinces of Siedlce and Lublin were obliged to accept Orthodoxy.[2] For the next thirty years, the policy of maintaining the enforced conversion of the Uniates to Orthodoxy was pursued by St. Petersburg; the strongest proponent of this policy was Konstantin Pobedonostsev, the procurator of the Holy Synod.

After the proclamation of the edict on religious tolerance, in April 1905, anywhere from 100,000 to 200,000 inhabitants of the two Polish provinces gave up Orthodoxy and became Roman Catholics of the Latin rite. The problem of nationality was complicated by the fact that not all the Poles were Catholics and not all the Ukrainians were Orthodox or Uniate. According to the official Russian statistics of 1906, the Orthodox population of the future province was 38 percent. Polish statistics, based on the official figures, numbered the Orthodox at 27 percent, whereas Henryk Wiercieński, the Polish expert, arrived at 25 percent for the Orthodox population and 57 percent for the Catholics. In any case, only in the district of Hrubieszów did the Orthodox population outnumber the Catholics.[3]

During the pre-constitutional era, the question of the separation of Chełm was actually raised eight times but was rejected by the government. The first plans were made in 1864 when the division of the Kingdom into provinces was being discussed. Nicholas Miliutin's assistant, Prince V. A. Cherkasskii, proposed that the creation of a province of Chełm would have a decisive effect on the "revival" of the

[2] Leon Wasilewski, *Dzieje męczeńskie Podlasia i Chełmszczyzny*, 2nd ed. (Kraków, 1918), pp. 6–10; Albert M. Ammann, *Abriss der ostslavischen Kirchengeschichte* (Vienna, 1950), pp. 523–31.

[3] Wasilewski, *Dzieje męczeńskie Podlasia i Chełmszczyzny*, pp. 58–59; *Rocznik statystyczny Królestwa Polskiego. Rok 1915* (Warsaw, 1916), pp. 6, 29, 32–33; Wiercieński, *Ziemia Chełmska i Podlasie*, pp. 7–12; Leon Wasilewski, *La paix avec l'Ukraine* (Geneva, 1918), p. 26.

oppressed Russian nationality that would otherwise be impossible so long as the area remained connected with the Polish centers of Siedlce and Lublin. But Miliutin opposed the scheme for financial reasons and also because out of a total population of 421,798, only 138,000 were Orthodox. He argued that as long as the Uniates were still subject to Rome, a new province would simply strengthen papal influence. Furthermore, the Russian population ought to enjoy full rights whatever the administrative divisions of the Empire, whereas the creation of the province might suggest that Poland still retained a special position. The question was dropped until the Uniate Church in the area was brutally liquidated in 1875, but another proposal in 1878 to separate the Bug region from Poland was disallowed. In 1882, the governor of Siedlce, supported by Pobedonostsev, suggested the separation of Chełm so that the governor of the province might concentrate on the problem of religious conversion. In 1889, the Orthodox bishop of the newly created diocese of Warsaw-Chełm, Leontius, in concert with Pobedonostsev, asked for the introduction of the Julian calendar into Poland and again raised the question of Chełm. These proposals were opposed by Governor General I. V. Gurko, who wished to keep the Uniates under his surveillance. He also preferred to preserve Chełm as a part of Poland in connection with the campaign of Russification, and he objected to the separation as a measure that would complicate military administration and strategy in view of the fact that the governors general were also commanders of the Warsaw Military District.

The Holy Synod constantly returned to the thought of separating the former Uniates from Poland, and Gurko's successor, Count P. A. Shuvalov, agreed to the idea of a separate province. However, he wanted it to remain under the jurisdiction of the governor general in Warsaw. On the other hand, his successor in 1897, Prince A. K. Imeretinskii, disagreed and I. L. Goremykin, the minister of the interior, was also opposed. Imeretinskii, who moved freely in Polish aristocratic circles, wished to avoid unnecessary dissatisfaction and friction. The governor of Lublin, Tkhorzhevskii, twice raised the issue of separation and, although backed by Pobedonostsev, was overruled by Imeretinskii and the latter's successor, M. I. Chertkov. In 1901, Chertkov stated that a clear national division was impossible in the provinces of Lublin and Siedlce, that other motives were "conjectural," and that financial support would be required for Russian institutions. The creation of a new province would be meaningless unless the government undertook a policy of Russification as thoroughgoing as in its northwestern and southwestern provinces. Consequently, he argued, it was enough to protect the Russian element from the Poles and Catholicism.

In 1902, D. S. Sipiagin, the crude and reactionary minister of the interior, summoned a special commission to discuss the question of Chełm, but the commission remained divided. Pobedonostsev pointed out that, despite the church reunion imposed in 1875, the mass of the population refused to attend Orthodox religious services. The creation of a new province was indispensable in order to protect and strengthen Orthodoxy and remove the population from the influence of Catholic Lublin and Siedlce. N. V. Muraviev, the minister of justice, emphasized in opposition that Chełm was part of the legal system of the governor generalship. Witte, the minister of finance, doubted the usefulness of a new administrative division since in all of Poland, as in Russia, the administration was in the hands of Russians anyhow and another division would not affect the lives of the inhabitants. Funds would be better expended

SIEDLCE

Biała

Bug River

Wieprz River

Włodawa

LUBLIN

Chełm

Bug River

Wieprz River

Hrubieszów

Zamość

Biłgoraj

Tomaszów

San River

▬▬▬ Boundary of the New Russian Province of Chełm

▬▬ Boundary between the Polish Provinces of Siedlce and Lublin

MAP 2. THE NEW RUSSIAN PROVINCE OF CHEŁM

in attaining more durable aims by subsidizing the Orthodox Church and religious institutions.

Sipiagin drew a distinction between the aims of Russian policy in Poland and in the western provinces. In the former, the aim was to protect Russians and former Uniates from Polish and Catholic influences. In the latter, the government desired complete Russification and the fusion of the region with Russia. The latter policy should also be extended to the area beyond the Bug River because of the allegedly "Russian" origin of its population. Furthermore, in order that the formal creation of a new province should be meaningful, the act must be accompanied by a series of measures designed to Russify the region. Poles should be forbidden to acquire property and Catholicism had to be repressed. "Perhaps" the Poles could be forcibly transferred to Poland in exchange for the Russian population remaining in the Kingdom. However, A. N. Kuropatkin, the minister of war, opposed an increase in the number of provincial administrative centers in border areas of the Empire as militarily inadvisable since plans for mobilization would have to be altered. Also, the economic dislocation and the effect on Polish opinion would make military administration even more complicated. Governor General Chertkov supported Kuropatkin because of the "complications" involved and added that it was essential to end all the rumors concerning the creation of a new province of Chełm.

The special commission concluded that a simple formal separation would be inadequate without actual measures of Russification, which were not possible under existing circumstances since unprovoked and harsh actions would lead to "an undesirable confusion of minds among the Polish population." Only in the course of years, after the population had been convinced that it belonged to the Russian people and the Orthodox Church, would the moment arrive to crown this process by separating Chełm from Poland. The emperor concurred in this conclusion.[4]

The situation was radically affected by the revolution of 1905. The pre-revolutionary autocracy had reacted hesitantly to suggestions, even from the powerful Pobedonostsev, for changes in the administrative machinery of the Empire. It had not been a particularly pressing concern whether or not Chełm was a part of the Kingdom because the Poles remained oppressed and no concessions to them were being considered. The government had considered itself strong enough not to have to fall back on debatable administrative changes in order to maintain its authority. Therefore, it had accepted the views and arguments of the local authorities.[5] But with the grant of certain civil liberties and the establishment of a constitutional system, whatever its limitations and drawbacks, the possibility presented itself that, sooner or later, Poland might wring a larger degree of self-government from St. Petersburg. The problem of Chełm thus acquired a greater urgency and Russian nationalists were concerned to limit as much as possible the area in which the Poles might assert themselves.[6]

Specifically, after the grant of the edict on religious tolerance in April 1905, the Orthodox clergy of Chełm, led by

[4] A. Zakrzewski, *Materialy k voprosu ob obrazovanii Kholmskoi gubernii* (Warsaw, 1908), pp. 1–6; see also L. Dymsza, *La question de Khelm* (Paris, 1911), pp. 121–31.

[5] A. Stakhovich, "Kholmskii vopros," *Russkaia mysl'* (March 1911), p. 100.

[6] In his memoirs, the assistant minister of the interior, S. E. Kryzhanovskii, referred to a proposal that he was working on at the time to revise the administrative structure of the Empire by dividing it into eleven regions that would enjoy broad local autonomy. One of these would be Poland. Kryzhanovskii was simultaneously preparing the bill to separate Chełm from Poland so that a new boundary might be drawn between Russia and Poland "in case" the administrative reform were adopted and Poland granted autonomy. See S. E. Kryzhanovskii, *Vospominaniia* (Berlin, 1938), pp. 130–34.

the vigorous Bishop Eulogius of the newly established and separate diocese of Chełm, was alarmed by the conversion to Catholicism of large numbers of former Uniates. In June 1905, Eulogius reported to the minister of the interior the extraordinary growth of Catholicism, and, in November, he led a delegation to the capital to warn of the danger of Catholic propaganda. The minister, P. N. Durnovo, raised the possibility of attaching some districts of the Bug area to the neighboring Russian provinces of Grodno and Volhynia. While N. A. Sukhomlinov, the commander of the Kiev Military District, agreed to the proposal, K. F. Krzhivitskii, the commander of the Vilno Military District, preferred the creation of a new province.

In March 1906, Durnovo presented to the Council of Ministers Eulogius' statements and those of the governors. He questioned the value of separating Chełm in order to preserve Orthodoxy, cast doubt on the possibility of Russification in border areas, and suggested that the economic dependence of the Russians on the Poles should first be ended. The governor general of Poland, G. A. Skalon, like his predecessors, argued against the idea of a new province as involving administrative and strategic complications that would outweigh any possible religious advantages, especially since the Orthodox population did not form a compact mass.

Finally, a special conference was held at the end of 1906 under the assistant minister of the interior, S. E. Kryzhanovskii. Among the participants was Bishop Eulogius, who was able "to interest" the emperor in the question.[7] The creation of a new province by utilizing Article 87 of the Fundamental Laws was proposed but, as a gesture to Skalon, it was also proposed that in military matters the new province be left under the authority of the Warsaw governor general.

7 *Ibid.*, p. 218.

The province was to preserve the existing legal system and tax structure but was to be subordinated administratively to the governor general and Court of Appeals in Kiev. However, in the light of social unrest, official unwillingness to arouse the Poles and undermine the loyalty of the moderates, and possible repercussions in the forthcoming Second Duma, the Council of Ministers in December 1906 decided to postpone action in order to prepare a bill that might be elaborated in connection with the proposal to introduce urban self-government in Poland.[8] It was to be expected that the concession of self-government would make the separation of Chełm less bitter for the Poles to accept.

The issue was taken up again by the Council of Ministers in 1907, and the Council finally decided, with the consent of the emperor, to have the necessary legislation drawn up. The task was entrusted to Kryzhanovskii and took two years to complete. According to Kryzhanovskii, while the bill was being prepared it was proposed that, as a certain compensation for the parts of the provinces of Siedlce and Lublin that were to be separated from Poland, there be joined to Poland some adjacent sections of the province of Grodno that were inhabited by Poles, specifically, a few localities in the districts of Bielsk and Białystok. But Stolypin would not agree to this proposal, fearing "attacks on the part of nationalist circles which would have considered inadmissible the cession to Poland of lands officially not belonging to it."[9]

The new province was to comprise six districts from the provinces of Lublin and Siedlce. The latter was to be abolished and its remaining western territory was to be incorporated into Lublin. No attempt was made to confiscate

[8] Zakrzewski, *Materialy k voprosu*, pp. 8–9; Dymsza, *La question de Khełm*, pp. 134–35.
[9] Kryzhanovskii, *Vospominaniia*, p. 135.

private property or introduce agrarian reforms, so that the existing social structure remained inviolate, that is, 536 estates would continue to account for 500,000 *desiatiny*, while 750,000 peasants owned 594,500 *desiatiny*.[10] Existing legislation, the Napoleonic Civil Code, and the nonclass communal structure were to be retained. The new province was to be judicially and educationally subordinate to the Kievan court and school districts but militarily subject to the governor general of Warsaw. State lands and properties were to be administered from Zhitomir, the capital of the neighboring province of Volhynia. The bill discriminated against Poles in various ways. The use of Polish was forbidden in private as well as public schools, in the courts, and in official correspondence. The Julian calendar was to be introduced. Poles from the Kingdom might not settle in the new province, and land might be purchased by Poles or Jews only from Poles. It was officially estimated that 304,-600 inhabitants, or 38 percent of a population of 758,000 in the new province, would be of the Orthodox faith. On the basis of nationality, there would be 406,000 "Russians" (the official designation for the Ukrainian natives) and 209,000 Poles. The bill was approved by the Council of Ministers and submitted to the Duma in May 1909.

After a short general debate caused by a protest declaration of the Koło, the bill was sent to a specially created subcommittee presided over by the Nationalist D. N. Chikhachev; the subcommittee worked on it for more than two years, so that the general Duma debates did not begin until November 1911. In the subcommittee, Kryzhanovskii explained the government's motives for introducing a bill to create a new province of Chełm. He stated that the thought had arisen in 1865 but had not been implemented because

---

[10] Figures from Mirosław Wierchowski, "Sprawa Chełmszczyzny w rosyjskiej Dumie Państwowej," *Przegląd Historyczny*, 1 (1966), 99.

of financial reasons and because the city of Chełm still had a small population of 4,000, while the urban center of Zamość was Polish in character. Furthermore, there had not appeared to be any urgency since it had seemed possible to safeguard the interests of the "Russian" nationality through general administrative measures. The reunion of the Uniates in 1875 with the official church had had a "formal" character, "had not penetrated the national consciousness" enough to wipe out the influence of the Union, and had also been opposed by Catholic influences. Kryzhanovskii conceded that the October Manifesto and the edict on religious tolerance of April 1905 had brought an "intensification of Latin-Polish propaganda" as well as "the abandonment of Orthodoxy by quite a significant segment of the Russian population and its conversion to Catholicism." Consequently, the idea of separation had come up again among the Orthodox population "in order to protect themselves against gradual engulfment by the advancing Latin-Polish element." Petitions had come from Chełm expressing the fear that, with the introduction of local self-government in Poland, the Poles would completely destroy the national self-consciousness of the Russian part of the population and subject it to the influence of the Polish proprietary class and Catholicism.

Kryzhanovskii admitted that the creation of a new province would not in itself guarantee "Russian national interests." A "permanent fusion" with the central provinces of the Empire would result only from a radical administrative, legal, and structural transformation of Chełm requiring many years. But the action of separation would encourage the Russian natives and check the Poles and Catholicism. Leaving matters as they were would mean "new successes" for Polonization. By contrast, after the separation, the Russian population would gain "new strength" to resist the "militant" Catholic clergy and the Polish gentry. Besides, since a large-scale administrative reorganization of local government throughout the Empire was being contemplated, it would be premature to consider drastic changes in Chełm until the reforms in the central provinces had assumed their final form. The separation would also facilitate reforms in Poland by eliminating the need for special measures to safeguard Russian interests.

The minister pointed out that, although the ancient historical boundaries of Chełm included almost half of Lublin and Siedlce, the new frontier should be moved east to include only areas "with a predominantly Russian population that has preserved the Orthodox faith and Russian language." His statistics indicated that the new province would have an Orthodox population of 304,885 and a Catholic one of 310,677. However, since the latter were in part Russian, having become Catholic "almost only since yesterday," the corresponding figures on the basis of nationality might be estimated to be about 406,000 Russians and 209,000 Poles. Kryzhanovskii's conclusion was that the new province would be "undoubtedly a Russian province." Finally, referring to the need for a "stronger local authority" and for an end to "religious and racial conflict," he urged that the province be placed under the governor general of Kiev. It might also be included in the Catholic diocese of Volhynia, the clergy of which "has relative moderation and less national fanaticism" than the diocese of Vilno, with its "extreme Polonism and excessive religious intolerance."[11] Kryzhanovskii refused to give the subcommittee the opinions of the five governors general in Warsaw regarding the separation of Chełm since four of them—Gurko, Imeretin-

[11] *Gosudarstvennaia Duma. Prilozheniia k stenograficheskim otchetam. 1910–1911 gg.*, V, No. 440, pp. 1–21.

skii, Chertkov, and Skalon—had opposed the project and only one, Shuvalov, had favored it. But this information was revealed by Dymsza of the Koło, and its authenticity was not denied by the minister, who was present.[12]

In its report, the subcommittee noted that in 1902 Witte had been against the creation of a new province because in Poland, as in the western provinces, the administration was in Russian hands. However, since that time, the official view had changed. In a meeting of the Council of Ministers in October 1909, Prime Minister Stolypin had stated that "if in the western region the Ministry sought to create a zemstvo with a Russian complexion, then, in the cities of the provinces of the Kingdom of Poland, we expect to see Polish self-government subordinate only to the Russian state idea."[13] Therefore, because of the threat to the Russian population, the subcommittee agreed with the government that the separation of Chełm from Poland was essential. On the other hand, the government's bill "was subject to strong criticism by the representatives of the Nationalist party who predominated in the committee" and insisted that the boundaries of the new province be extended. Kryzhanovskii was present in the committee as the representative of the government, "but since Stolypin's orders were not to oppose the wishes of the Nationalists, I had to keep silent."[14]

The Nationalists and Rightists in the subcommittee contended that the government's bill did not succeed in giving the Orthodox population of Chełm a majority. They also argued that religion was not a clear or exact criterion of nationality because of the extensive conversions to Catholicism after 1905, the economic dependence of the peas-

[12] Stakhovich, "Kholmskii vopros," p. 76.
[13] *Gosudarstvennaia Duma. Prilozheniia k stenograficheskim otchetam. 1910–1911 gg.*, V, No. 440, p. 115.
[14] Kryzhanovskii, *Vospominaniia*, p. 136.

antry upon the gentry, and the fact that profession of Catholicism did not necessarily mean Polish nationality. Consequently, it was proposed to include in the new province all places "with a significant Russian population," both Catholic and Orthodox, as well as Orthodox religious centers and areas with "cherished historical memories" for Russia. Also, smaller administrative units of district and commune should not be divided. A final desideratum was that the province should have a "convenient figure." The boundaries recommended by the committee were averred to have an advantage over those proposed by the government in that the configuration of Chełm would be "more rounded and less broken." The effect of this recommendation was to increase the population of the province from 758,000 to 898,000. This would mean 463,900 "Russians" and 268,000 Poles; 327,300 Orthodox and 404,600 Catholics. These statistics were challenged by the Poles on the committee but were accepted by the Nationalist-Rightist bloc.

The Duma's subcommittee introduced other modifications into the government's bill. The preservation of the governor generalship of Kiev was termed "extremely undesirable." It no longer served a purpose since the southwestern provinces, acquired by Russia after the partitions of Poland in the eighteenth century, no longer differed essentially from the neighboring ones. They, like the province of Chełm, should be directly subject to the Ministry of the Interior. Chełm might preserve the Siedlce court system, which the government bill had abolished, the existing civil and commercial laws based on the Napoleonic Code, and most criminal laws. However, the new province was to be subordinate to the Educational District and Court of Appeals of Kiev.

The government's bill was liberalized by the subcommittee only in matters of property and language. The motivation was obviously to guarantee Octobrist support. The Octobrists on the committee were willing to accept the bill as a measure designed to restrain the Polonization of Chełm but were anxious to pay some regard to the principles of the October Manifesto by toning down several of the manifestly anti-Polish aspects of the bill. The committee rejected the government's proposal to extend to Chełm the law of May 1, 1905, for the nine western provinces of Russia that allowed Poles to acquire land from Poles but not from Russians. Since Russian land ownership in Chełm was slight, the committee concluded that the proposal had little practical significance, was "pointless," and would arouse "dissatisfaction" in moderate Polish circles. On the other hand, Polish immigration into the new provinces from Poland would be allowed only with the permission of the governor in order "to preserve the province from the excessive influx of people who might prove undesirable in view of the goals being pursued by the establishment of the new province."

The committee also did not agree to exclude the Polish language completely from the courts. A limited use was allowed before justices of the peace and in communal courts —in order not to discourage possible conversions to Orthodoxy. Also, as against the government bill, the committee allowed the teaching of Polish in those intermediate schools that had a majority of Poles, because these students were usually in the largely Polish towns where there was no need to safeguard the Russian nationality. The prohibition of such instruction would be regarded, in addition, by the population "as an aggressive attack on the Polish nationality." On the other hand, apart from this concession, the laws and regulations allowing the teaching of and instruction in

Polish that applied to Poland and the western provinces were not to obtain in the new province, where the rules for the central Russian provinces were to be introduced.[15]

The plenary discussion of the bill by the Duma began on November 25, 1911; the committee report was delivered by Chikhachev. He emphasized the contention of the Nationalists that in Chełm the ethnographic data did not correspond with those of religion and that "the Russian population speaking the Little Russian dialect" was the predominant element. He drew a connection between the separation of Chełm and the bestowal of local self-government on Poland, because "the sole way of facilitating the introduction of urban and rural self-government is to separate the Russian part of the Kingdom of Poland." He stated that the subcommittee had rejected the governmental proposal on the limitation of Polish land ownership "out of considerations of exclusively practical expediency." Chikhachev also referred to the charge that the bureaucrats of the old preconstitutional order had rejected as harmful and pointless the proposal to separate Chełm. He deplored their satisfaction with half-measures and their inability to see the question of Chełm as one of national significance. By contrast, the Duma, as a representative institution, was able to pursue "a consistent and systematic national policy."[16]

Chikhachev's address was supported by Makarov, the arrogant minister of the interior, who pointed out that, despite the historical arguments, the matter was not one of an international territorial disagreement, that "Poland is not a state but part of the Russian Empire," and that the essence of the issue was the necessity of preserving the national consciousness of the Russians in Chełm and their

---

[15] *Gosudarstvennaia Duma. Prilozheniia k stenograficheskim otchetam. 1910–1911 gg.*, V, No. 440, pp. 109–59, 193.
[16] *GDSO, 1911–1912 gg. Sessiia* V, I, 2601–2608.

feelings of loyalty to the Russian state. Makarov also spoke in favor of restrictions on the right of Poles and Jews to acquire land as a necessary measure "in defense of the Russian people living there."[17]

The principal speaker and the initiator of the bill was Bishop Eulogius, who was actively supported by the Nationalist stalwart, V. A. Bobrinskii. Eulogius took up Makarov's argument. "We fully believe that in the entire expanse of our great state, from Kalisz to Vladivostok, there is no Kingdom of Poland, but only a single Russian state." Indeed, the term "Kingdom of Poland" was "an archaism" without any "real significance." Bobrinskii attacked the policy of Alexander I and of the bureaucrats in the second half of the nineteenth century as one that had preserved the dependence of the Russian peasant upon his Polish lord with the result that more Russians had been Polonized in the past hundred years than during three hundred years of Polish rule. Both speakers emphasized that the economic subordination of the peasantry of Chełm was more significant than administrative reforms and that the next step must be one of organized assistance by the state. Representatives of the Rightists, like Markov and F. F. Timoshkin, criticized the bill in the committee version as too moderate. They charged that its terms and reservations and its concessions to the Poles fostered the illusion that a Kingdom of Poland existed as a separate entity, while the bill gave no protection to the Russian peasantry from the oppression of the Polish gentry. They advocated forcible population transfers and the adoption of a program of systematic and thorough Russification.

No other issue discussed by the Duma aroused more activity on the part of the Koło than the Chełm bill. The Poles, like their opponents, had recourse to prolonged historical

[17] *Ibid.*, pp. 2608–20.

disquisitions in order to demonstrate the ancient ties that bound Chełm to Poland. They pointed to the long and successful activities of the Roman Catholic Church in the area. They criticized the historical material and fabricated statistics used by the government. They insisted on the impossibility of drawing a boundary in such a racially and religiously mixed area. They spoke of the organic links between Chełm and Poland and warned of the administrative, economic, and cultural chaos that would result from the passage of the bill. They deprecated the inflammation of nationalist passions. The tactics of the Poles were essentially defensive and aimed at the preservation of the status quo in Chełm.

In line with the Polish parliamentary program of restraint and moderation, the Koło maintained the hope that by cooperating with the Duma center, avoiding conflicts with the government, and opposing radical schemes of social reform, the loyalty of the Poles would be rewarded by modest concessions that might, in the course of time and with the further liberalization of Russia, be broadened in scope. This hope was brought out in Grabski's remarks, which also referred to the anti-Russian demonstrations that were occurring in Galicia. He declared that, unlike the revolutions of 1830 and 1863, the revolution of 1905 in Poland had been not a national but a "social revolution." Also, after 1905, anti-Russian sentiments were on the wane, the Poles accepted Russia's new structure of government, and the German threat was coming to be regarded as the main challenge to the Polish cause. However, the current nationalist policy of the Duma as represented by the bill on Chełm was cutting the ground from under the feet of the Polish deputies in the Duma who accepted the Russian state.

On the question of Chełm, as on all questions of nationalism, the Octobrists were split. During the plenary discussion, G. V. Skoropadskii and V. A. Potulov spoke in favor of the separation. The former insisted that "the moral support" which the Russian peasant would receive from the passage of the bill would have "vast significance." The latter added that, although it was asserted that the separation would arouse the hatred of the Poles, the last four years of the Duma had proved "that Polish hearts burn with hatred of everything Russian." Although the right wing of the Octobrist party intended to vote for the bill, the initiative for its passage remained in the hands of the Rightists and the Nationalists. On the other hand, the Progressives and the Kadets clearly expressed their negative reactions to the government's bill. Speaking for the Progressives, Uvarov, the erstwhile Octobrist, brushed aside the official statistics as tendentious compilations. He rejected the project as one of no value either to the administration or to the local population but as one that would simply affront the "sensitive nationalism" of the Poles. He pointed out the obvious inadequacy of the city of Chełm as a provincial capital. He emphasized the administrative confusion that would result from having educational and judicial control in Kiev and the administration of state lands and properties in Zhitomir. The law code was to remain Polish, but appeals had to be made to Kiev which was unfamiliar with the code. Uvarov went on to say that warnings of the supposed danger of Polonization were sheer pharisaism and that Orthodoxy could easily be protected within the existing provincial structure. The Kadet Rodichev stated that the formula "Russia for the Russians" merely meant places and privileges for Russian bureaucrats. "Polish nationalism is that of the oppressed; your nationalism, that of the oppressors." Luchitskii noted that the separation of Chełm would signify no change that might benefit the Ukrainian peasantry, and he was seconded by the Social Democrat N. S. Chkheidze, who termed the life of the Ukraine "one continuous trage- dy" and who asked, "In what way is Russification better than Polonization?" V. A. Maklakov accused the bill of being "without content" and charged that it would only create "an exclusive patrimony (*votchina*) for the Ministry of the Interior." He also warned that the narrowly con- ceived nationalism of the government would strengthen German influence among the Slavs.

On January 20, 1912, when the vote was to be taken for a second reading of the bill, Von Anrep spoke for himself and those Octobrists who agreed with him, including Nicholas Khomiakov, the liberal former president of the Duma. He opposed the bill and concurred with Maklakov that it was without content. "Introducing nothing positive, it intro- duces a good deal that is negative." At the same time, he cautioned that it would give "completely unfounded hopes to the Poles," namely, the hope of eventual Polish autono- my. The separation of Chełm would leave the Congress Kingdom ethnically homogeneous and might lead the Poles to expect excessive concessions as compensation. Although Von Anrep was shouted down by the right, he was able to state that, despite all kinds of promises that were being given by the rightist parties to the Poles concerning the re- forms that the Kingdom would be granted after the separa- tion of Chełm, he was certain that the Duma would "very much have to think carefully before implementing such promises as are being given here at random."[18]

The second reading of the bill by articles was accom- panied by the same stormy debates as had been the open-

[18] Ibid., pp. 2650–66, 2675–92, 2694–2711, 2729–47, 3159–73; II, 319–31, 255–69, 504–509, 266–69, 143–54, 465–73, 473–504, 523–28, 625–32, 643–59, 717–19, 722.

ing discussion. A proposal by Rodichev to include in the new province only localities having an Orthodox population of no less than 40 percent was rejected. A later proposal of his, at the third reading, to adopt the boundary recommended in the original government bill was also voted down. The Duma also rejected an amendment by the Progressive N. N. Lvov to draw the provincial boundary on the basis of religious statistics because statistics on nationality were prejudiced and unreliable. A furor was created by Article 10 of the bill "to separate the newly formed province of Chełm from the provinces of the Kingdom of Poland and subordinate it in general administration to the Ministry of the Interior." This article was twice voted down, possibly because enough Octobrists felt that the wording was an unnecessary affront to the Poles. In any case, Articles 11 and 12 that dealt with the process of separation were passed and, at the third reading, Article 10 was voted with the phrase "to remove the province of Chełm from the administration of the governor general in Warsaw."[19]

Taube, the assistant minister of education, addressed the Duma on the matter of restricting the use of Polish in the schools and urged that it was "logically necessary" for Chełm to be included within the general school system of the Empire. But the Duma accepted an Octobrist motion to preserve the school laws operative in Poland, and the school language restrictions of the bill were rejected. The assistant minister of justice, A. N. Verevkin, protested the provisions of the bill allowing the limited use of Polish in the proceedings of justices of the peace and communal courts because "the entire purpose" of the bill was "the gradual fusion of the province of Chełm with central Russia and the protection of the local population against dena-

[19] *Ibid.*, II, 1903, 1928–29, 2187; III, 3371.

tionalization." The Duma, however, agreed to the use of Polish in the lower courts and also accepted the provision that Poles be allowed to acquire land. On the other hand, it passed the article allowing Polish migration only with the permission of the governor.

At the end of the third reading, the bill was passed by the Duma in essentially the committee version on April 26, 1912, by a vote of 156 to 108. The Rightists G. A. Shechkov and S. V. Voeikov expressed indignation that only the eastern parts of Siedlce and Lublin were being separated, rather than the entire provinces, thus leaving the Russian population of the western districts "under the yoke" of the Poles. They also protested the right of Poles to acquire land and deplored the fact that the bill did not free the Russian population of Chełm from dependence upon the Polish gentry. Speaking for the Kadets, "the genuinely elected representatives of the Russian people," Rodichev dismissed the bill as a measure of national and religious oppression. Von Anrep regretted that the bill was simply an irritant that provided no benefits to the native Russian population.[20]

The bill was sent to the State Council where it was passed with a rapidity totally uncharacteristic of that chamber, from June 11 to June 14, 1912, so that the measure might become law by the summer of that year. The pressure, urgency, and impatience with opponents of the bill were such that several members of the committee, chaired by P. P. Kobylinskii, refused to consider the project within the narrow limits prescribed by the chairman and left the committee. M. G. Akimov, the president of the State Council, also refused to allow the chamber to discuss Kolybinskii's actions. The reporter of the committee was the reactionary Pikhno. He declared that Chełm was "without any doubt" Russian, that the boundaries were drawn "care-

[20] *Ibid.*, II, 2681–84, 2719–25; III, 3408–09, 3412, 3413–15.

fully and conscientiously," and that there were no "substantial inconveniences" in the creation of the new province. Makarov addressed the upper house and attributed all the uproar over the bill to "Polish chauvinism." He referred to the "state significance" of the measure and indicated that it was merely the first step in bringing Chełm close to "Russian principles." The Pole Szebeko complained of the statements being made "loudly and bombastically" about a united and indivisible Russia. Meysztowicz expressed the hope that the geographical shape of "a boot" presented by the new province would be avoided if certain localities with a Polish population in the majority were excluded, but this proposal was voted down. The Council also rejected a motion by the Polish industrialist Stanisław Rotwand that Chełm remain subject to the Warsaw Court of Appeals rather than come under that of Kiev because of the retention of the Napoleonic Code. An attempt to eliminate the article allowing Polish immigration only with the consent of the governor was likewise defeated. The bill was passed on June 14.[21]

The passage of the bill to separate Chełm from Poland was the crowning action of the Third State Duma in its handling of the Polish question. It demonstrated clearly that whenever any issue involved nationalist sentiments, whatever the facts, merits, or statistics of the case, the Duma would have a conservative majority. While the smaller left wing of the Octobrists might be restrained by conscience or principle, the center and right wing of the party would vote with the Nationalists and the Rightists. This was illustrated by a remark made by Guchkov in a newspaper interview: "The question of Chełm is a question of honor for the Poles and for Eulogius. Please do not be

[21] *GSSO. 1911–1912 gg. Sessiia VII* (St. Petersburg, 1912), pp. 4902–4908, 4959–69, 5158–60, 5182, 5197, 5202.

133

surprised that the honor of Bishop Eulogius is dearer to us."[22] Octobrist ambiguities were also revealed in an exchange between S. I. Shidlovskii and Miliukov during a debate over the budget of the Ministry of the Interior on March 16, 1912. The Octobrist stated that nationalism should be a formula uniting all citizens of the Empire and establishing honorable conditions of existence for all of them. The unity of the state had to be preserved, but internal relations ought to be based on justice or there would never be domestic peace. The Polish question, in particular, had to be approached "with some circumspection" because of the Poles' culture and traditions, "and there is no reason whatsoever to attack these traditions for nothing and unnecessarily." Miliukov replied that the Chełm bill was hardly an example of "circumspection," and he feared that the hopes placed by the Poles in the Octobrists would be deceived.[23]

Indeed, the outcome of the matter was a severe blow to the Poles and to their belief that a spirit of loyalty and cooperation would help them to win modest concessions from the Duma or at least, as in the question of Chełm, would guarantee maintenance of the status quo. The Koło opposed the bill persistently and fiercely but from a carefully defined position of loyalty to the Russian state and hostility to the idea of revolution, whether national or social. Its members expressed regret at being obliged to go into opposition and even dissociated themselves from the anti-Russian demonstrations being staged in Galicia. However, they were disappointed. While the final version of the bill did preserve in Chełm many existing institutions, the social structure, and certain rights for the Poles, it was to be expected that in the future a policy of Russification would be pursued so that

[22] Quoted in Wierzchowski, *Sprawy Polski*, p. 182.
[23] *GDSO. 1911–1912 gg. Sessiia V*, III, 1409–13, 1513–14.

134

the new province would be incorporated into the central provinces in more than a formal administrative fashion. Furthermore, if the Kingdom of Poland were to be granted rights of self-government, the territory of their application would be much reduced, and the ties between Chełm and the other areas of Poland would become further attenuated.

It should be added that, despite the fact that there was a new head of the Council of Ministers after the assassination of Stolypin, the attitude of the government during the prolonged Chełm affair remained unchanged. Although the bill had originated during the prime ministership of Stolypin, the debates on it began in the Duma two months after his assassination in Kiev, in November 1911. The new prime minister, Kokovtsov, was not at heart an advocate of the official nationalist course. At Stolypin's grave he spoke the words, "Enough of nationalist rhetoric; now conciliation is necessary."[24] He also took action to forestall any pogroms against the Jews. In Kiev, he was visited by a delegation of Nationalists from the Duma headed by Balashov and Chikhachev. They referred to Stolypin's close connection with the party and sympathy for its ideals. However, they added that the party did not have confidence in Kokovtsov because it feared that his policy would be "completely different, foreign to clear national ideals, permeated by excessive sympathy towards the West, and, consequently, towards foreign elements . . . ." The Nationalists stated that they could not support him unless he assured them that he would carry on Stolypin's policy.

Kokovtsov reacted with some heat to this demand, whereupon the Nationalists said that they would support him if he would give not necessarily "assurance" but merely "hope" that he would adhere to Stolypin's policies. After pointing out that Stolypin's influence had been on the wane

[24] Izgoev, "Ot tretei Dumy k chetvertoi," p. 191.

after the zemstvo crisis and that "no amount of support" by the Nationalists could have saved his political career, Kokovtsov declared that he would never be the "plaything" of any party, but that if the Nationalists' motto really was the greatness of Russia, then agreement between them and the government was simple. "But I do not share, and cannot serve, your policy of oppressing foreigners. This policy is harmful and dangerous. . . . To persecute today a Jew . . . then a Pole, a Finn, and to see in all of them enemies of Russia whom it is necessary to curb in every way, with this I do not sympathize and will not go along with you."[25]

However, although Kokovtsov was honorable and intelligent, he lacked the command, drive, and forceful personality of his predecessor. From the beginning, his position was weaker than Stolypin's had been at court, within the cabinet, and in the Duma. Kokovtsov's first appearance before the Duma was to defend a governmental project dealing with factory medical funds, but in his second appearance he defended Stolypin's nationalist Finnish bills and stated the principle of the "continuity" of cabinets. In a speech for which he received an ovation from the right and center, including the Nationalists, as well as a telegram of congratulations from the emperor, Kokovtsov referred to the "expectation" that every successor had to be in opposition to, or at least in disagreement with his predecessor. But in questions affecting "the vital interests . . . the integrity and unity of the state, its glory and power, in all the fundamental questions of the satisfaction of the vital needs of the Russian people, there must not be hesitations and disagreements on the part of the successor . . . ." Kokovtsov stated that, as Stolypin's successor, he had to defend "with the same conviction" the nationalist projects that had been introduced in the legislature by Stolypin. "Russian legisla-

[25] Kokovtsov, *Iz moego proshlago*, I, 483–86.

tion" ought to embody a "just appreciation" of the Russian nationality.[26] Thus, the fears of the Nationalists proved to be unfounded, and Kokovtsov followed Stolypin's nationalist course by pursuing to their enactment the bills on Finland and Chełm.

[26] *GDSO. 1911–1912 gg. Sessiia* V, I, 694–95.

VII

URBAN SELF-GOVERNMENT IN POLAND

THE BILL to extend to the cities of Poland the municipal self-government act of 1892 was a practical necessity. However, it was elaborated by the government at the same time as the bill on Chełm and appeared to be an attempt to compensate the Congress Kingdom for its loss of Chełm.[1] Like the question of the separation of Chełm, the issue of local self-government for Poland had a long history. The proposal had been raised first by the viceroy of Poland, Berg, in 1870, the same year that municipal regulations had been introduced in the central Russian provinces as part of the social reforms of Alexander II. However, nothing had been done either then or in 1892, when Alexander III issued new regulations enlarging the authority of the provincial governors over the organs of urban self-government.

At the end of 1906, the government revealed its intent to carry out the reform, and in 1909 the Council of Ministers created a committee on local economic affairs whose purpose was to prepare a bill to introduce urban self-government in Poland. At the first meeting of the commit-

[1] A. S. Izgoev, "Politicheskaia zhizn' v Rossii," *Russkaia mysl'* (Jan. 1912), p. 5.

tee, on October 15, Stolypin referred to the issue of the zemstvo institutions in the western provinces. He stated that the government's intention in the zemstvo bill was "to safeguard Russian national principles in a multinational area of Russia." However, in the self-government bill for a country that was predominantly Polish, the aim was "to protect the political rights of the state, to insure the new institutions against attempts to obtain autonomy for Poland, and to give Russian citizens, independently of the will of the majority, the right to participate in the administration of urban self-government." Stolypin went on to say that while the Council of Ministers desired the zemstvo institutions in the western region to have a Russian "complexion," it expected to see in the cities of the Polish provinces Polish self-government that would merely be subordinated to "the Russian state idea." However, the government had to face the necessity of enfranchising apartment owners because the Russians in Poland were mostly not owners of real estate. Furthermore, there had to be three electoral curias —Polish, Russian, and Jewish—because otherwise the Russians would be excluded from city administration while Jews could acquire "predominance." Jews were not to number more than one-fifth of the town councilors.

Stolypin also enunciated a new principle upon which governmental supervision of the councils would be based: that the government could judge the legality but not the advisability of the councils' actions. This meant that the broad discretionary powers of interference enjoyed by the administrative authorities in Russia over municipal government as a result of the reactionary law of 1892 would be narrowed and defined. Governors would be left the right to carry out, at the expense of the cities, any municipal obligations that the councils might refuse to acquit. The government would also retain the right to dissolve the councils before their term expired. In addition, "in view of the border location of the Polish cities and the possibility of political complications," the Council of Ministers proposed to give the government the right to replace the system of self-government with the former direct administration for a period of no more than three years, each time with special imperial approval. The Polish language might be used in internal business matters by the councils, but Russian was to be used officially. Stolypin concluded by repeating that the proposed measure would grant the Polish population the self-government "to which it has the right because of its high native culture but without any thought of turning self-government into a weapon of political conflict or a means of attaining political autonomy." He also mentioned the intention of the Council of Ministers to introduce a second bill to create institutions of rural self-government in Poland.[2]

The governmental bill was presented to the Duma by the Ministry of the Interior on May 29, 1910, and was referred to the committee on urban affairs. The bill departed from the municipal regulations of 1892 in extending the franchise beyond owners of real estate of a certain qualifying value and large commercial and industrial enterprises to include all owners of real estate as well as apartment owners who paid city taxes as well as the state tax on apartments. The voters were to be divided into three curias to elect the town councilors: the first for Russians, the second for Jews, and the third for "the remaining residents." In order to insure Russian representation on the town councils, the Russian curia might elect one councilor if there were at least five voters in the curia. By contrast, if Jews composed

[2] *Gosudarstvennaia deiatel'nost' predsedatelia soveta ministrov statssekretaria Petra Arkadevicha Stolypina* (St. Petersburg, 1911), I (1909 i 1910 gg.), 21–25.

more than half the population of a city, they had the right to elect no more than 20 percent of the councilors. If they numbered less than half, they might elect no more than 10 percent, but only 10 if they themselves constituted no fewer than 10 percent of the city population. By comparison with the regulations of 1892, the number of councilors was increased and might be anywhere from 30 to 160. The chairman of the council was to serve for one year, had to be approved by the government, and might not be a Jew.

All transactions between the city administration and the government had to be conducted in Russian. All documents not composed in Russian in the original had to have a Russian translation. In the internal administration of the town councils, all documents and records had to be in Russian. Translations into Polish were allowed but had to be accompanied by the Russian text, which was the official one. Oral declarations in the councils might be made in Russian or Polish. Decisions and instructions of the city administration had to be published in Russian or in Polish with an accompanying Russian text. Governmental supervision over the activities of the councils was narrowed by comparison with the regulations of 1892 and was preserved only in connection with the legality of the acts of the city administration. The government, in line with Stolypin's outline of the bill, preserved the right to fulfill lawful municipal obligations that the councils failed to honor, to dissolve the councils before their term of office had expired, and to replace them with direct governmental administration.[3]

The Duma's committee on urban affairs modified the governmental bill in several ways. The tax qualification for apartment owners was reduced so that the number of Russian voters would be increased. The committee approved

[3] *Gosudarstvennaia Duma. Obzor deiatel'nosti gosudarstvennoi Dumy tret'iago sozyva*, II, 106–109.

the curial principle because, even if a certain number of Russians had to be members of the city councils, the non-Russians would choose those who would "serve their interests" or be "insignificant" and without influence, while the Russian voters would have no voice in choosing either Polish or Russian representatives. The committee dropped the provision that chairmen of city councils and their assistants might not be Jews and rejected the stipulation in the government's bill that baptized Jews were to be included in the Jewish curia. It accepted the provision that the council might be dissolved before its term of office had expired but proposed that a new council had to be assembled within a period of two months.

Furthermore, while the councils might be replaced by direct governmental administration because of "the necessities of state," the period should be no longer than two years rather than the three proposed by the government's bill. Also, such action ought not to be "a general measure of administration" but one taken only for "exceptional circumstances" affecting each city separately. Finally, the committee defined more exactly than did the government's bill the right to use Polish. All internal transactions of the city administration "requiring governmental supervision" had to be recorded in Russian. The prescription that all resolutions and decrees of the city council that were made public had to have a Russian as well as Polish text was changed by the committee to mean only those that were required to be made public "according to the law."[4]

The debate on the bill began in the Duma on November 23, 1911. P. B. Sinadino, a Nationalist from Bessarabia, was the committee reporter. He defended the committee version of the bill and pointed out that it signified the

[4] *Gosudarstvennaia Duma. Prilozheniia k stenograficheskim otchetam. 1910–1911 gg.*, III, No. 217, pp. 3–20.

first recognition of the right to use Polish publicly in official gatherings. However, the question of national curias aroused the greatest interest among the speakers that followed. Count E. P. Bennigsen spoke on behalf of the Octobrists in favor of the bill. He approved of the creation of a Russian curia, and his party opposed completely equal rights for the Jews that would give them "total mastery" of the cities. Speaking for the Progressives, Uvarov supported the bill despite its "dark sides." He stated that he would introduce amendments to replace the curias with a system of proportional representation and to give the right to vote to the Christian clergy.

The Poles, who had strongly opposed curias in the western zemstvo bill, now accepted them. Their acceptance without protest of restrictions on Jews led to an open breach between them and the Kadets. This breach contributed to the rather lukewarm support given the Poles by the Kadets in the matter of the separation of Chełm that was being debated by the Duma at the same time. Grabski read a declaration from the Koło that although the bill was not completely satisfactory because of the narrow rights granted for the use of the Polish language, the government's right to dissolve the councils, and the danger of the reimposition of administrative control, nevertheless it constituted a "vast improvement" over the existing urban administration. Jaroński declared that the bill would be "unthinkable" without limitations on Jews. Full rights would lead to a Jewish inundation of the city administrations so that the Jewish question, "already bitter among us, would become unbearable."

The Social Democrat T. O. Belousov declared that he would vote against the bill because its aim was "to stir up national passions." Alekseev introduced a resolution that the chairman of city councils had to conduct the meetings in Russian. The resolution was accepted by the Duma, and a motion by Grabski at the third reading of the bill to have this requirement dropped was rejected by the chamber. The government representative, N. N. Antsiferov, opposed the slight committee alterations in the articles on language. He declared that the government's bill insisted that Russian had to be official in all aspects of the transactions of the city councils. However, the Duma's committee had limited this proviso to activities subject to governmental supervision; therefore, some internal transactions, "however insignificant," were excluded. Antsiferov's objection to the use of Polish also applied to the published resolutions and decrees of the councils because of "the very nature of the institution as an organ of administration." On the other hand, he accepted Alekseev's motion. Antsiferov's objections were voted down by the Duma.[5]

The curial question continued to be debated during the second reading of the bill on November 28. Belousov voiced the negative attitude of the Social Democrats toward the concept of national curias. He attacked the current nationalist course in Russia as "merely a mask assumed by stupid chatterers, venal publicists, and calculating exploiters of genuine human passions." He also attacked the Koło for accepting curial restrictions on the Jews while the Poles themselves were suffering in their representation in the Duma from the system. He deplored "zoological instincts" and urged the Poles to be guided by the principle of equality for all rather than by that of the ends justifying the means. The historian I. V. Luchitskii labeled the curias a form of "divide and rule," while N. N. Shchepkin, also a Kadet, charged the Poles with having lost "the awareness

[5] *GDSO. 1911–1912 gg. Sessiia* V, I, 2429–59, 2499–2500, 2510, 2764, 2789; II, 1708; I, 2766–67, 2789.

of truth and justice." However, the Progressive proposal to eliminate curias in favor of a system of proportional representation was voted down. Rightist motions by Markov to eliminate the Jewish curia and by Timoshkin to reintroduce in the government's bill the clause that converted Jews be included in the Jewish population were likewise turned down.

The Kadets, Labor Group, and Octobrists introduced motions to drop from the bill Article 188 which, in the committee version, allowed the government the right to replace the elective city administration for up to two years by the administration of the government. In this way, the Duma conceded to the government two out of three control rights included in the original version of the bill: fulfillment of municipal obligations and dissolution of the councils before the expiration of the term of office, but not replacement of the elective administration. Despite the defense of Article 188 by the government's representative and Sinadino, the Octobrists and the opposition in the Duma rejected it, 120 to 65. It was again rejected at the third reading.

The Duma, however, over the protests of the Poles, accepted the motion of the Lithuanian A. A. Bulat that in the province of Suwałki, the use of Lithuanian, rather than Polish, be allowed alongside Russian in the internal deliberations of the councils. Motions were accepted to extend the franchise to the Christian clergy and to women owning real estate. However, Grabski's proposal to allow the members of one curia to propose candidates and vote for councilors in other curias was defeated. Finally, an attempt by the government to restore the provision that the chairmen of the councils and their assistants might not be Jews was defeated. The bill was passed on the third reading on February 6, 1912, by a majority of the Octobrists and the right wing. The left wing, the Kadets, and a majority of the Progressives voted against it.[6] The measure on urban self-government was first discussed by the State Council on December 4 when N. A. Zinoviev, one of "the most active figures of the rightist group"[7] and a former provincial governor in Poland, objected to municipal regulations that would give the Kingdom "such rights which are not granted to the inhabitants of the Empire." He stated that, in Russia proper, apartment owners were excluded from the franchise, except in St. Petersburg. Moreover, even in the capital the percentage of voters was small. Furthermore, although the bill passed by the Duma was designed to enfranchise Russians, the Russians in Poland belonged to "the more substantial" classes, and the relatively low qualifying tax requirement would, in industrial cities like Łódź, turn municipal government over into "the hands of mere workers."

The bill was then returned to committee. It was brought before the chamber again on April 3, 1913, with Zinoviev as the reporter. The committee concluded that it opposed special municipal regulations for Poland despite the "inadequacies" of the law of 1892. The law ought to be reformed for the entire Empire after a general investigation. Meanwhile, the existing law should be retained with changes demanded by local circumstances. The curias had to be preserved in order to safeguard the Russian population and prevent the Jews from dominating the councils, which the committee "under no circumstances desired." The committee "of course" did not agree to the Duma's very low tax requirement. However, it was prepared to accept the use of spoken Polish and Lithuanian as "necessary." The commit-

[6] Ibid., I, 2834–37, 2839, 2849, 2860, 3242, 3247; II, 1708, 1716, 1722.
[7] A. D. Stepanskii, "Politicheskie gruppirovki v gosudarstvennom Sovete v 1906–1907 gg.," Istoriia SSSR, 4 (1965), 53.

tee preserved the provision of the law of 1892 dealing with governmental supervision, and it restored the article providing that the maximum length of time for which town councils might remain dissolved be kept at three years. The committee also fixed the time limit at six months rather than two for new elections should a council be dissolved before the term of office had expired.[8] The representative of the Ministry of the Interior accepted the report of the special committee.

However, the Rightist A. S. Stishinskii raised the question of language as "the most significant" one in the bill. In the city councils, attempts by Russians to have debates translated would arouse a "hostile attitude" on the part of Poles and Lithuanians, as well as charges of "obstruction." The consequence would be an "exacerbation" of mutual relations. Besides, knowledge of the Russian language in Poland was "adequately diffused among the local urban population." The use of Polish would be "the first step" in the direction of curtailing the use of Russian in urban administration elsewhere in the Empire. This would be so in light of "the striving of the non-Russian nationalities inhabiting our borderlands . . . towards national self-determination that is now manifesting itself." Stishinskii declared that elective institutions of local self-government would create a Tower of Babel in the twentieth century. Furthermore, "all of history" has demonstrated the "strong tie" of a state language in unifying various nationalities within a single state.

The Pole Szebeko replied to Stishinskii and warned that it was not "in the interests of the Russian state," particularly at that time, to create such conditions of life for the Polish population on native Polish soil that would estrange it from the belief that its "better future" should always be

[8] *GSSO. 1912–1913 gg. Sessiia VIII*, pp. 152–53, 1373–80.

connected with the Russian Empire. He referred to the possibility of conflict between "two worlds," the German and the Slavic. If these two worlds were to clash, all the Slavs should be united in one of them and, for Russia, there was only one course of action—conciliation of its fellow Slavs. Szebeko's indirect appeal for a Russo-Polish reconciliation on the basis of Russian concessions to the Poles was attacked by V. I. Gurko as a "threat." In the end, the State Council rejected the use of Polish. Meetings of the city councils were to be conducted by their chairmen in Russian, and all transactions, records, and oral statements were required to be in Russian.

With regard to the tax qualification, Durnovo suggested that apartment owners be enfranchised only in Warsaw since a general application of the principle in Poland would entail its extension to Russia. He urged that the slight advantage of a few more Russian councilors weighed less in the scale than "the harm" in giving the vote to apartment owners in all of Russia. His motion was rejected, 63 to 62, but the State Council accepted Zinoviev's proposal to increase the tax qualification. Another rightist, A. A. Naryshkin, considered that the Jews, "a nationality without a fatherland" that nursed "an irreconcilable hatred towards the Christian world," should not be given the right to elect council members. Jewish members should be appointed and not exceed 10 percent of the membership of the councils. However, the State Council defeated this proposal and accepted the Duma's version of this article. The State Council also passed the article allowing the government to disband city councils ahead of time, but it restored the time limit of two months for new elections as against the committee's recommendation of six months.

The Council rejected, 55 to 53, the committee's proposal that the system of elective city government might be suspended by the government for up to three years. On the other hand, it did pass Article 50 allowing the authorities to dissolve a city council not as a general measure but for special reasons affecting any city individually and with the stipulation that the reasons must be made public at the time that the action was taken. The bill as a whole was passed by the State Council on April 5, 1913, and was sent back to the State Duma.[9]

The report of the Duma's committee on urban affairs noted that the upper and lower houses had disagreed on the three issues of the franchise, language, and governmental supervision. The State Council had observed that the grant of urban self-government in other borderlands of the Empire meant simply the application of the general laws of the country without special regulations. A distinct statute for Poland would be incompatible "with the union of the borderlands with the central provinces." The Duma committee disagreed with the Council because of the "inadequacies" of the law of 1892 and because its direct application to certain borderlands did not in itself justify the extension of the law to others. In addition, the aim of uniting the borderlands to the central provinces of Russia could hardly be attained simply by extending to the former the laws of the latter. Also, earlier extensions of the applicability of the municipal regulations of 1892 had been to individual cities, not to an entire country. Finally, the question of a general urban reform that had been raised by the Council was not relevant because no proposal for such a reform had been presented by the government to the legislature.

With regard to the franchise, the report of the committee on urban affairs observed that although the State Council, "exclusively out of considerations of policy in the border-

[9] Ibid., pp. 1384–96, 1405, 1448, 1452–56, 1464, 1488–92, 1517, 1523–24, 1531, 1550.

lands," had preserved the franchise for apartment owners, it had almost doubled the tax qualification in general and had almost tripled it for Warsaw. The committee proposed a compromise figure. Female owners of real estate and clergymen, except those who were Orthodox, were not to be enfranchised. In the problem of language, the committee insisted that Polish be allowed in oral declarations, but it proposed that the chairman of the city council be obliged to summarize statements in Russian should anyone request it. The report noted that the State Council had not accepted the Duma's version of governmental supervision whereby the authorities might supervise only the legality of the acts of the city administration and not interfere with its activities in the sense of their "advisability." The committee, however, called attention to the fact that the government itself, in its bill, had rejected the old forms of supervision. Such supervision would simply permit the local authorities to interfere constantly in various secondary activities of the elective institutions inasmuch as important decisions had to be confirmed by the governor or the Ministry of the Interior. Furthermore, the purpose of the government's bill had been actually to extend the competence of the new bodies by comparison with those of the central provinces. Therefore, the committee recommended that the attempt of the State Council to expand the supervisory powers of the authorities over the city councils be rejected by the Duma, particularly in view of the fact that the government had adequate control over the councils at any time.[10]

The bill was returned from committee on June 5, 1913, and Bennigsen, the Octobrist, was the reporter. He repeated the arguments in the committee report and em-

[10] *Gosudarstvennaia Duma. Prilozheniia k stenograficheskim otchetam gosudarstvennoi Dumy. Chetvertyi sozyv. 1912–1913 gg. Sessiia I* (St. Petersburg, 1913), III, No. 331, pp. 1–9.

phasized that the condition of the cities in Poland was "lamentable" and that it was "essential to do something." Because a rejection by the Duma of all the changes made by the State Council would lead to "the complete collapse" of the bill, Bennigsen urged that, out of "purely utilitarian considerations," the Council's version be essentially accepted with the exception of the changes made by the committee on urban affairs. A motion to hasten passage of the bill by restricting debate was opposed by the Progressive A. M. Maslennikov because of the complexity of the issue and because of the danger of "servility" to the State Council. However, the Koło accepted the restriction. Dymsza declared that if the bill were not passed before the approaching end of the session, it would be postponed at least a year. Józef Świeżyński stated that the Duma's bill was not quite satisfactory but that it was acceptable to the Poles in terms of "stern reality" and as "a first step" to further reforms in the Kingdom. However, the exclusion of Polish by the State Council was "unacceptable" and, by comparison with this change, all the others were "secondary." Świeżyński added that limited governmental supervision was also desirable because, while supervision under the law of 1892 was "onerous" in Russia, in Poland it would be such that "there would be no limits to arbitrariness."

The Kadet Shchepkin reverted to the theme of the "subservience" of the Duma to the wishes of the State Council as expressed in the recommendation of the committee on urban affairs. He argued that the result would be to make the Duma simply a consulting body to the Council. "You were sent to legislate, not to lackey." For this outburst, Shchepkin was excluded from five meetings of the chamber. Rodichev, the Polish expert of the Kadets, declared that the bill would introduce not peace but a sword in Poland. He protested the restriction on debate in the Duma and charged the Poles with supporting injustice and violating the principles on which their own claims were based. In another address, Rodichev reproached the Poles for their subservience to the State Council and for their attitude toward the Jews, and he reminded them of Chełm and the western provinces. He stated that Polish autonomy should not mean denial of the rights of the minorities in Poland. The impulsive and shallow Alexander Kerenskii violently denounced the tactics of the Koło in limiting debate as "the greatest crime possible in a parliament." He attacked the Polish delegates themselves as "traitors to their people." He was subsequently deprived of the floor.

The break between the Poles and the Kadets became painfully evident during the debates on June 12. The specific reasons were the acceptance by the Koło of the State Council's version of the bill, with the alterations recommended by the Duma's committee on urban affairs, of the restriction on debate, and, without protest, of the extremely limited franchise for Jews. The speech by Rodichev, the former Polonophile, urging the Poles not to oppress their minorities prompted a reply delivered by Harusewicz. He asserted that the Poles had not given the Kadets the right to teach them lessons in political behavior, particularly since the Poles had shown such marked restraint in the Duma. He pointed out that the Kadets had supported the introduction of zemstvos into the provinces of Astrakhan, Orenburg, and Stavropol despite franchise restrictions with regard to property and nationality. He accused the Kadets of not understanding the Poles and of "the most vulgar kind of doctrinairism." Stating that "we shall not sacrifice our own existence . . . for the most sublime doctrine," Harusewicz made his final rejoinder to Rodichev by quoting the lines of the poet Lermontov: "Our love was without joy; our parting will be without sorrow" (*Była bez radosti liubov'; razluka budet bez pechali*). Rodichev answered indignantly by accusing the Poles of "blindness" in cooperating with the right wing by means of "casual alliances." By a vote of 145 to 45, with the left wing in the minority, the Duma passed the committee version of the bill on the third reading.[11] A critical comment in Warsaw was: "In the lower house, the left attempts to reject the reform; in the upper house, the conservative right attempts to make it impossible of acceptance and normal functioning."[12]

The bill was reconsidered by the State Council on November 27, 1913. The upper house was addressed by Prime Minister Kokovtsov himself on the subject of the language provisions "so that the point of view of the government would be clear to the State Council on this subject and so that there would be no doubts about this." The prime minister stated that the government supported the Duma version of the bill. The local population did not have a mastery of the Russian language. "To be sure, this fact must be deeply regretted," but it had to be taken into consideration. A refusal to allow use of the native language would limit the effectiveness of those elements whose efforts were necessary to the success of the measure. Kokovtsov rejected the charges that the bill was unfair, favored one border area, prejudiced other border areas, and marked a departure that threatened to disrupt the unity of the state and would result in a "federation of separate localities." He spoke of the "cohesion" in race and language of the urban population of Poland and asked whether there were not "certain signs of justice" in allowing within modest limits the use of Polish for oral statements in the city councils. The government believed that, in order to attain the principal goal, it was

[11] *GDSO. 1912–1913 gg. Sessiia I* (St. Petersburg, 1913), III, 959–72, 977, 991–92, 1290–1300, 2067–71, 2078–82, 2106–2107.
[12] "Kronika miesięczna," *Biblioteka Warszawska* (July 1913), p. 189.

correct to allow, "even if temporarily," that concession regarding the Polish language which the government had proposed and which the Duma had further restricted. Without this concession, in the opinion of the government, the very possibility of introducing municipal regulations would be subject to the greatest doubt.

Kokovtsov referred to the Baltic provinces where urban self-government had been introduced in 1877; the German language had been admitted on an equal level with Russian only to be completely replaced in 1889 by Russian. "Perhaps we will find the opportunity of acting exactly as we acted twelve years after the initial introduction of municipal regulations in the Baltic area," and perhaps there might be even a shorter interval in Poland. The prime minister concluded by saying that although it was "natural" for the vast majority of the members of the State Council to dream of the time when all the Slavic streams would flow into the Russian sea, the government was faced with the question under what circumstances the Polish stream would the sooner flow into that sea. Because the Poles were "not yet prepared to the necessary degree" to apply the law of 1892 unconditionally, a limited use of the native language had to be conceded.[13]

Despite his nationalist rhetoric, Kokovtsov was mistrusted by the nationalists because of his obvious reservation. A group of rightists in the cabinet intrigued against him and cooperated secretly with the right wing of the State Council. Like his predecessor, Kokovtsov was opposed by the court camarilla and was losing the confidence of the emperor and empress. He was to be dismissed from office two months after his vain appeal to the State Council. Indeed, when the vote was taken, I. G. Shcheglovitov, the

[13] GSSO. 1913–1914 gg. Sessiia IX (St. Petersburg, 1914), pp. 101–109.

minister of justice, N. A. Maklakov, the minister of the interior, and A. V. Krivoshein, the minister of agriculture, remained absent from the upper house, thus making public the schism within the cabinet.[14]

Stishinskii immediately replied to Kokovtsov's arguments with the heated and fanciful statement that an attempt was being made "to raise Polish to the rank of a second state language" and to introduce "Polish self-government without subordinating it to Russian principles of state." He went on, saying that Polish leaders would not be satisfied with the slight concession that was contemplated but would demand further concessions in the schools, courts, and administration, and "finally, perhaps, Polish legislative assemblies." Zinoviev accepted Kokovtsov's statements on language and declared that, in a dozen years, knowledge of Russian would be widely diffused in Poland. Szebeko pointed out the preferential position that Russian would enjoy immediately. Meetings of the city councils had to be conducted by the chairmen in Russian. All written transactions had to be in Russian. Anyone had the right to speak in Russian, and every non-Russian speech had to be translated on demand. Gurko attacked Kokovtsov's statement on the temporary use of Polish. "I ask myself what this is: naiveté or simple provocation?" Any attempt at a later date to exclude the use of Polish would certainly create indignation and a loud reaction.

When the vote was taken, the State Council once again rejected any use of Polish. With Kokovtsov in the minority, the language article in the Duma's bill was defeated, 94 to 74. The higher tax requirements in the Council's bill were also restored, and the Council's definition of the govern-

[14] A. S. Izgoev, "V zakonodatel'nikh palatakh," *Russkaia mysl'* (Dec. 1913), p. 4.

ment's supervisory rights was again substituted for that of the lower house.[15] In its action, the State Council ignored the protest of Governor General Skalon who, in a special memorandum to the emperor, advocated the use of Polish in the system of self-government so that extremists would not be able to use this fact for purposes of agitation. The vote was also a heavy blow to Kokovtsov's prestige and position, and it strengthened the hand of the rightist opposition to him both at court and in the upper house of the legislature. In any case, if the bill were eventually to be passed with the restriction that Russian alone might be employed by the future city councils of Poland, it was noted that the result would be the creation of "new branches of the Berlitz schools for the high life of the cities."[16]

A conference committee of both houses of the legislature convened in February 1914 to discuss the bill and attempt to reach agreement on the three main discrepancies in the two versions. The representatives from the Duma sought, without success, to place the issue on a high level by urging the necessity of insuring the loyalty of the Polish element on Russia's western frontier. However, the representatives from the upper house were more concerned about administrative uniformity. The two sides finally agreed on the tax qualification when the Duma members accepted a slightly raised figure for the smaller cities. The representatives of the State Council held to their position that the municipal regulations of 1892 should go into effect and that the administration retain the right to supervise not only the legality but also the advisability of the decisions of the city councils. A majority of the members of the conference com-

---

[15] *GSSO. 1913–1914 gg. Sessiia IX*, pp. 110–15, 120–24, 139–52, 158–61, 182, 197; A. Shingarev, "Zemskoe i gorodskoe samoupravlenie," *Ezhegodnik gazety Rech' na 1914 god* (St. Petersburg, 1914), pp. 218–19; I. Clemens, "Pol'sha," *ibid.*, pp. 252–53.
[16] "Kronika miesięczna," *Biblioteka Warszawska* (Nov. 1913), p. 392.

mittee finally accepted the Council's version of this article, and the Duma members who agreed to it did so "in order to give the present bill an opportunity of passage." However, efforts to reach agreement on the matter of language once again ended in failure. The seven delegates from the State Council were adamant in refusing to endorse the view of the seven delegates from the Duma that the use of Polish be allowed in debates but that the chairman be obliged to speak in Russian and translate into Russian on demand.[17]

The bill was debated in the Duma on March 27. Speaking on behalf of the Koło, Świeżyński announced that the Poles would accept the conference committee's compromise on the tax requirement as well as the article on administrative supervision in the version of the State Council "in order not to hinder the realization of the bill." However, despite the importance of the reform for Poland, the insistence of the State Council that Polish be totally excluded from the deliberations of the city councils was unacceptable. Alekseev and Zamyslovskii retorted by defending the sole use of Russian as the state language. The latter also protested the exclusion of the Rightists and Nationalists from the conference committee by a left-center majority in sympathy with the Poles. He recalled that the entire left wing had voted against the bill as a whole but that now the Octobrist center was supporting the left on the language issue in the committee. Bennigsen replied that the State Council had chosen as its representatives on the conference committee only those whose point of view was that of the majority of the Council in the vote on the bill. Consequently, the Duma had been obliged to choose as its representatives those whose point of view on the language provision reflected the opinion of the majority of the Duma. Zamyslovskii an-

[17] GDSO. *1913–1914 gg. Sessiia II*, III, 298–99.

nounced that the Rightists would abstain from voting on the committee's report. With 34 abstentions, the Duma voted, 173 to 30, to accept the points on tax qualification and supervision in the version recommended by the majority of the conference committee and the point on language in the version last passed by the lower chamber. The final vote on the entire bill was 151 to 84, with the extreme right and left in the minority.[18]

The bill was discussed by the State Council for the last time on May 12, 1914. The chamber was addressed by the new prime minister, the indolent and timeserving Goremykin, who was supported by all of his ministers as his predecessor Kokovtsov had not been.[19] As a nominated member of the right wing of the Council, Goremykin had earlier voted against the bill. His current advocacy of it reflected the fact that the highest authorities wanted the bill to pass.[20] Even the minister of foreign affairs, S. D. Sazonov, was involved. In connection with Balkan developments, he had sent a memorandum to the emperor demonstrating that the position of the State Council was causing Russia to lose the sympathy of the Balkan Slavs and, by contrast, was raising the stock of Austria-Hungary among them and especially among the Poles. In view of Russia's extremely tense relations with Austria-Hungary, such an anti-Polish policy was extremely short-sighted and fraught with serious consequences.[21] Beginning with the phrase, "By the will of the emperor," Goremykin referred to the burden on his "weakening shoulders." He stated that the government was obliged "to stand firmly" on the position that it was adopting. The State Council "has done its work" and, with the exception of the one point on language, the Duma had ac-

[18] *Ibid.*, pp. 299–305, 310, 312, 328.
[19] K. Arseniev, "Khronika," *Vestnik Evropy* (June 1914), pp. 350–51.
[20] "Kronika miesięczna," *Biblioteka Warszawska* (July 1914), p. 188.
[21] Avrekh, *Tsarizm i tret'eiiun'skaia sistema*, p. 100.

ceded to the position of the upper house. Therefore, the government found it necessary to stand on the side of the Duma in the matter. The State Council had no "adequate reason" to oppose the lower house and the government and "to place serious obstacles" in the way of the bill. But Goremykin's appeal availed nothing. The Council rejected the language article, 87 to 71, and the bill was defeated.[22]

Despite the careful moderation of the Koło, the conciliatoriness of the Duma, and the strong final support of the government, the State Council saw fit to reject a bill of far-reaching significance on the basis of a single point: the right of Poles to speak Polish at meetings of city councils. Despite the passage of fifty years after the January uprising of 1863, and despite the broad institutional transformation of Russia after the revolution of 1905, it was clearly shown that conservative and nationalist elements retained the strength to prevent any meaningful changes for the better in official policy toward the minorities. It was also demonstrated that the loyalist and cautious tactics of the Polish conservatives in the Duma were successful in prying from the Duma only the most meager concessions and from the State Council not even these whenever the chord of official nationalism was touched. On June 5, 1914, an imperial rescript to the prime minister instructed him to introduce the bill in the Duma once again and, on June 9, this was done by the Ministry of the Interior. However, the outbreak of war precluded any further legislative action. A last echo of the issue was the promulgation, under Article 87, of urban self-government in Poland by the Russian government in 1915—four months before the occupation of Warsaw by the German army.

The hopes of the Poles to obtain concrete concessions from the Third Duma by the pursuit of a policy of sustained

[22] *GSSO. 1913–1914 gg. Sessiia IX*, pp. 2081–82, 2131.

moderation were ultimately frustrated. The support of the Kadets was occasionally limited by the relatively conservative approach of the Polish Koło to social and economic questions. Although the general program of the Octobrist center was not unsympathetic to moderate Polish aspirations, legislative proposals embodying specific ameliorations of the standing of the Poles within the Empire invariably split the party into a right and left wing. The result was that the Octobrists supported the legislation on the western zemstvos, elementary education, and Chełm but introduced minor modifications designed to make these bills slightly less disagreeable to the Poles. On the other hand, although the Octobrists voted for the bill on urban self-government for Poland, even this concession to the Poles was hedged with restrictions and reservations. The emergence of the Russian National party in the third session of the Duma, 1909–1910, and the tendency of Stolypin to push a nationalist policy to appease the right and regain his waning influence at court indicated that even the virtues of prudence and moderation would avail the Poles little against the current of official Russian nationalism.

VIII

THE FOURTH DUMA AND THE POLISH QUESTION
IN THE YEARS 1912–1914

TOWARD THE END of the fifth and last session of the Third
Duma, Guchkov commented on the Polish question in an
interview given to the Polish newspaper *Świat*. His remarks
illustrated the temporizing tactics of his party and revealed
the rather unpromising prospects for Russo-Polish relations
in the Fourth Duma. He stated that the Octobrists in the
Third Duma had wanted to do "somewhat more" for the
Poles and had had in mind parallel Russian and Polish
courses at the Russian university in Warsaw. However,
Stolypin had not approved this suggestion, although "he
defended himself weakly." Guchkov went on to say that
the Octobrists had nevertheless thought that they would
have convinced Stolypin had he lived. The Octobrist leader
asked that the Poles give his party "further credit." He
declared that, "as a beginning," the Poles should be granted
everything "to normalize their social life" and, above all,
should have removed from them "the restrictions preserved
from the past." Guchkov admitted that the Octobrists had
"unfortunately" not worked out a detailed plan for the
gradual improvement of Russo-Polish relations and that
this task had to be performed by the next Duma.[1]

[1] As quoted in *Rech'*, May 17, 1912.

The elections to the Fouth Duma were characterized by vigorous intervention on the part of the government in behalf of the right-wing elements. Huge official subsidies were employed; pressure was brought on the Orthodox clergy to participate vigorously; and many attempts were made to disqualify or defeat opposition candidates, including left-wing Octobrists. Guchkov himself was defeated in Moscow. The principal result of the elections was a great weakening of the position of the Octobrists, whose representation dropped from 148 at the first session of the Third Duma to 99 at the first session of the Fourth. The parties to the left gained a few seats, but the parties to the right increased the number of their delegates to 185. There was a further increase in the number of Great Russian deputies over the national minorities. The number of Ukrainians was cut from 25 to 10, of Belorussians from 12 to 6, and of Poles from 18 to 16. The Polish-Lithuanian-Belorussian group was reduced from 7 to 6 and the Koło from 11 to 9.[2] Except for the election in Warsaw of a Socialist deputy, Eugeniusz Jagieł-ło, the political complexion and much of the composition of the Koło remained the same.

In view of the fact that Polish grievances had received slight satisfaction in the Third Duma with its large Octobrist center, the political configuration of the new Duma with its strengthened right wing was a guarantee that even less conciliation could be expected in matters involving Russian nationalism. Kokovtsov's policy statement on December 5, 1912, was intentionally colorless and general and avoided "acute questions of principle."[3] However, he assured the assembly that the basis of Russian political life

[2] "Vybory," *Ezhegodnik gazety Rech' na 1913 god* (St. Petersburg, 1913), p. 234; W. B. Walsh, "The Composition of the Dumas," *Russian Review*, 8 (April 1949), 115.

[3] Kokovtsov, *Iz moego proshlago*, II, 133.

would remain "the unity and indivisibility" of the Empire and the preservation of the "first place" of the Russian nationality and the Orthodox faith. He added that this view did not preclude a favorable official attitude toward those nationalities "that recognize Russia as their fatherland . . . and consider their welfare and even their very being to lie in union with the great Russian nationality."[4] Although Kokovtsov went beyond a simple request to the national minorities that they fulfill their obligations to the state and urged them to regard Russia as their "fatherland," his remarks about the position of the Russian nationality annoyed the right wing as too moderate. He was attacked during the debate for his "inadequate support of nationalist demands and complete disregard of Stolypin's legacy." Kokovtsov himself considered that it was the purpose of the right wing "to make my position difficult."[5] Purishkevich was particularly outspoken. He referred to increasing separatist tendencies in the border provinces of the Empire and declared that the prime minister's appeal for concord sounded ironical. He asserted that war would break out with Germany and Austria, the Poles would organize an uprising, and, consequently, the government ought to pursue an energetic and firm policy of control.[6]

Speaking on behalf of the Poles, Marian Kiniorski expressed "feelings of deep disappointment" with the "abstract phrases" of Kokovtsov's address. He insisted that the government was deliberately ignoring the "vast political importance" of the national question, that the speech was the best proof that everything remained as before, and that the government had no positive program with regard to the Polish nation. Worse, the issue was not merely the absence

[4] *GDSO. 1912–1913 gg. Sessiia I*, I, 260–81.
[5] Kokovtsov, *Iz moego proshlago*, II, 134.
[6] *GDSO. 1912–1913 gg. Sessiia I*, I, 286–312.

of a program but rather "the notorious impotence of the governmental authorities" that were unable to pursue a positive course in domestic politics. Solemn promises of reform were devoid of any practical significance, and an actual regression was to be observed—back to the former policy of no concessions in language or self-government.

Kiniorski asserted that the course of the Third Duma had "completely confirmed the pessimistic view" of the Koło. The Poles had participated in the Third Duma, despite the unjust reduction of their representation, "with the aim of defending the interests of our nation even in the limited area of reforms" that was open to them. But both the government and the legislature had persisted in ignoring the reforms recognized as urgent in 1905. Kiniorski pointed to the fate of the bill on self-government in the State Council, the issue of Chełm, and, despite Kokovtsov's promises, the dismissal of Poles from the Warsaw-Vienna railway line. Therefore, the Poles found themselves obliged to reject official rhetoric in the light of "all-consuming" Russian nationalism. "At the present moment, we see no signs attesting to a change in the political system that has striven up to now, if not for the complete extermination of the Polish nation, then in any case for a reduction of its vital forces." Kiniorski pointed out that none of the parliamentary activities of the Poles could possibly be regarded as hostile to the interests of the state. He concluded that if the government refused to accept the idea of an autonomous structure for Poland, the Poles had the right to expect the government to work out another program that would at least guarantee the normal development of the Kingdom.[7]

Nevertheless, the only significant legislative proposal in the Fourth Duma concerning the Polish question was the bill to introduce urban self-government, and the fate of that

[7] *Ibid.*, pp. 349–56.

bill was decided by the upper house of the legislature. Despite the tense international situation and the growing possibility of armed conflict between Russia and the German powers, the weak and divided ministries of Kokovtsov and, to an even greater extent, Goremykin were patently unable and unwilling to produce any program of broad reforms that might insure the loyalty of the Poles. Within the Duma, the powerful right wing remained adamant in its hostility to the national minorities and in its refusal to conciliate them. The Octobrist center was in greater disarray than it had been during the Third Duma and more than ever divided into a left and a right wing. The mood of depression and frustration was expressed by Guchkov at the Octobrist party congress in November 1913. He spoke of governmental paralysis and the shift in the political center of gravity in favor of the forces of reaction. He referred to the loss by the government of "its light constitutional hue as well as the idea of a united cabinet." He warned that the traditions of the autocracy were acquiring a new lease on life after the failure of Stolypin to check the resurgence of reactionary forces. "Now, looking back on the short but instructive political path that we have traversed, we must admit that the attempt made by Russian society . . . to reach an accord with the authorities . . . has suffered failure . . . . The attempt of Octobrism to reconcile these two externally hostile forces—the state and society—has failed."[8] Nevertheless, with regard to the Polish question, the Octobrists continued to urge the Poles to remain loyal to Russia and maintained the vague and nugatory formula of "equal rights" for the Poles within the Empire.

Speaking for the Kadets, Miliukov criticized Kokovtsov's opening address for its appeal to the minorities not merely

[8] A. I. Guchkov, *Rechi po voprosam gosudarstvennoi oborony i ob obshchei politike 1908–1917* (Petrograd, 1917), pp. 98–106.

165

to cooperate with the government but also to regard Russia as their fatherland. Referring to Kiniorski's statement that the Poles were loyal to the state but would not renounce their patriotism, Miliukov commented, "I welcome both this moderation and this proud refusal."[9] Kokovtsov then replied to Kiniorski's declaration and expressed surprise that the Poles felt that they were subject to oppression and injustice.[10]

In the debates on the budgets of the various ministries, representatives of the Koło voiced familiar grievances. The pointlessness of the official policy of Russification in the Polish school system was emphasized. Attention was called to the subordination of the courts to the police. It was pointed out that Poles living in the western provinces of Russia were still subject to the legal restrictions introduced after 1863. It was again noted that Poland paid higher taxes than did Russia proper and had a railway system inferior to that in advanced areas of the Empire. However, these anticipated protests aroused little interest in the center and right majority of the Duma. The predictable attacks by the right on the Poles that had characterized the history of the Third Duma were usually missing in the Fourth Duma. Conceivably, the conflict in the Balkans and the threatening international situation also worked against noisy demonstrations of Polonophobia.

The interpellations introduced by the Polish deputies in the Fourth Duma dealt mostly with secondary and local problems: difficulties in the development of private schools in Poland, an instruction of the minister of education that the nationality of students was to be determined by school officials, various attempts by the authorities in the western

[9] *GDSO. 1912–1913 gg. Sessiia I*, I, 603.
[10] *Ibid.*, pp. 672–74.

provinces to harass the Roman Catholic clergy and remove the Polish language completely from public signs, and the mass dismissals of Polish employees from the Warsaw-Vienna railway line.[11]

The general mood of apathy toward Polish problems in the second session of the Fourth Duma was suddenly and dramatically dispelled by the July crisis of 1914 and the outbreak of World War I. A one-day special session of the Duma was summoned on July 26 to vote war credits. At this session, Jaroński delivered a brief but emotional address on behalf of the Koło. He spoke of the historic moment when Slavdom and the Germanic world "led by our ancient foe, Prussia" were about to enter into fatal collision. He described as tragic the position of the Polish nation deprived of its independence and the possibility of demonstrating its free will. Poland would not only be a theater of war but also, divided into three parts, would witness its sons fighting on hostile sides. However, despite this division, Jaroński went on, the Poles ought to be as one in their "feelings and sympathies towards the Slavs." They should be prompted in this not only by the justice of the Russian cause but also by "political intelligence." The world significance of the moment should relegate to the background "all domestic scores." He voiced the hope that Slavdom "under the leadership of Russia" would deliver a rebuff to the German powers comparable to the one that had been administered to the Teutonic knights five centuries earlier by Poland and Lithuania at the battle of Grunwald in 1410. Jaroński concluded with the fervent wish that the blood to be shed by the Poles as well as the horrors to be experienced by them in what would be for them a fratricidal war would

---

[11] "Kronika miesięczna," *Biblioteka Warszawska* (May 1913), pp. 338–89; (Aug. 1913), pp. 398–99; (July 1914), pp. 189–93.

"lead to the union of the Polish nation torn into three parts." He received an ovation from the right, center, and left of the chamber.[12]

The theme of Grunwald was taken up in the proclamation to the Polish nation issued on August 1, 1914, by the commander-in-chief of the Russian army, Grand Duke Nicholas. Russia "trusts that the sword that beat the foe at Grunwald has not rusted." The proclamation also spoke of the "fraternal reconciliation" of Poland with Russia. It asserted that the boundary lines which divided the Polish nation would be obliterated and that the Poles would be "reunited under the scepter of the Russian Tsar." On the other hand, the proclamation specified that Russia expected from the Poles "an equal regard" for the rights of the nationalities with which history had linked the Poles. Furthermore, although the proclamation declared that, under the Russian scepter, Poland would be "reborn, free in her faith, language," the original wording that had promised the Poles autonomy was replaced by the weaker and more ambiguous expression of "self-government."[13] Thus, the Russian government essentially promised Poland unification and the establishment of self-government under the scepter of the Russian emperor.

However, it soon became evident that Russian policy in Poland did not change appreciably as a consequence of the Grand Duke's proclamation. The only significant concession made to Poland by the imperial government during the entire war was the promulgation of the urban self-government act. This gesture, however, proved a disappointment in view of the expectations aroused among the Poles by the proclamation of August 1, 1914. The imperial

[12] *GDSO. 1913–1914 gg.*, 26 VII 1914, p. 21.
[13] Frank Golder, ed., *Documents of Russian History 1914–1917* (New York, 1927), pp. 37–38.

government missed the opportunity of taking advantage of the cooperative attitude of many Poles. It finally disappeared from the historical scene without having carried out even its modest promises to Poland.[14]

[14] Alexander Dallin, "The Future of Poland," *Russian Diplomacy and Eastern Europe 1914–1917* (New York, 1963), pp. 1–77.

IX

THE FATE OF POLISH NATIONALISM
WITHIN THE RUSSIAN EMPIRE

THE IRONY of Russian history in the early twentieth century was that although the revolution of 1905 succeeded in modifying the autocracy and in opening the way to limited constitutional government, the spirit of extreme nationalism throughout Europe, as well as the continent's interlocking system of permanent alliances, was driving the Russian Empire into war and self-destruction. This irony was clearly reflected in Russian approaches to the renewedly important Polish question.

By the beginning of the century, the theme of insurrection that had dominated and embittered the Russo-Polish relationship during much of the nineteenth century was considerably muted by the passage of time and Polish economic progress within the Empire. In addition, many influential Polish political leaders were confident that Russia's new parliament would legislate reforms in Poland. This confidence was fortified by increasing apprehension with regard to Wilhelminian Germany with its mounting persecution of the Poles in Germany and its generally aggressive and expansionist policies. As the danger of armed conflict between the central powers of Germany and Austria-Hungary and the Franco-Russian allies increased, the Poles in the State Duma might reasonably have expected that Russia would alter its hostile policies toward its Polish subjects. Such a change in policy would have made sense, certainly, in view of the possibility of an international clash that would find Polish loyalties divided among the three powers.

Even though it was obviously desirable to secure Polish loyalty to the Russian state by granting necessary and long overdue reforms in Poland—which might even attract the Poles in Germany and Austria-Hungary to Russia's side—Russian policies and attitudes toward Poland during the period 1905–1914 did not change substantially from the pre-constitutional pattern.

Close examination of the treatment of the Polish question by the State Duma throws considerable light on several aspects of Russian political life during the last years of the Empire. The efforts of the Polish delegates to obtain redress of the most conspicuous Polish grievances illuminate the workings of the Russian legislature and political parties. Many typical Russo-Polish attitudes of the early twentieth century are reflected in the parliamentary debates. It was a period of deepening political reaction. The Duma's handling of the Polish problem reveals graphically not only the strong nationalist current that affected a broad spectrum of opinion in Russia, but also the Russian political system's response to and handling of the nationality question in general. Furthermore, because the Poles in the Duma regarded themselves as the spokesmen of their entire nation and were therefore disinclined to enter into close and binding ties with Russian political parties (though they did frequently form various temporary alliances for tactical purposes), relations between Russians and Poles in the Duma tended to be direct and uninhibited. The upshot was that the Poles found themselves abandoned.

The broadest claim made by the Poles in Russia after the failure of the revolution of 1905, that of political autonomy in a kind of revival of the Congress Kingdom of 1815, died with the first two brief and turbulent Dumas. Moreover, even Russian liberals, then and later, were often reticent and hesitant when rhetorical generalities had to be converted into specific reforms. Some, like Miliukov, were suspicious of Polish aspirations and apprehensive of the possible consequences of a political decentralization of the Empire. With the change of the electoral law on June 3, 1907, and the convocation of a conservative Third Duma, the situation worsened for the Poles, and their representation in the legislature was radically reduced. The Koło's policy of moderation and loyalty toward the Russian state and tactical cooperation with the Duma's center brought no significant legislative results and also aroused the displeasure of the opponents of the regime.

The Kadets favored greater social and economic radicalism than did the Poles; further, the Kadets remained fearful of the supposed consequences of Polish nationalism and, on doctrinal grounds, disapproved of the flexible tactics of the Poles, who wanted positive accomplishments legislated for Poland by the Duma. The Octobrist center was a loose grouping. Its position was hesitant and, in the final analysis, negative. Its theoretical program of granting Poles equal rights with Russians within the Empire was vitiated in practice by the timidity of the party's leaders and the consistent inclination of the party's sizable right wing to follow nationalist dictates. The nationalist course in the Third and Fourth Dumas was overtly and unrestrictedly directed by a

Rightist-Nationalist combination upon which the government came increasingly to rely.

Stolypin himself was perhaps only anti-Polish regarding the western provinces of Russia, but the Nationalist party on which he came to count put less of a fine point on the matter. Furthermore, Stolypin's own position was steadily undermined by rightist intrigues at court and in the State Council. Kokovtsov, although less of a nationalist than Stolypin, did not have the prestige and strength of character of his predecessor. He too was weakened by rightist opposition, and while the bill to separate Chełm from Poland went through the legislature, the simultaneous effort to give Poland urban self-government with a minimal use of the Polish language was frustrated by the upper house. Most significantly, the government had no carefully thought out or worked out program for the Polish question and, as Russian relations with Austria-Hungary steadily deteriorated after the Bosnian crisis, increasing and censorious comparisons were drawn between the ways in which the Poles were being treated by the Romanovs and by the Habsburgs. Sazonov particularly wanted to satisfy the reasonable demands of the Poles in order to secure their loyalty to Russia, but nothing was undertaken by the government in the last days before the war. Despite the threatening international situation, the weak government followed a policy of drift and was unable to overcome rightist parliamentary opposition to the mildest reforms in Poland. During its brief existence, the Russian legislature introduced no new or positive elements into the somber relationship of Russians and Poles. The negative factors were too many. An alteration was to come only under the radically different circumstances of Russian military defeat and domestic revolution.

This study has shown that, despite the threatening international situation and despite the creation of a legislative assembly in the Empire, next to nothing was accomplished in the way of improved treatment by Russia of its Polish population. Deep and traditional Russo-Polish antagonism, a narrowly conceived Russian nationalism that infected not only the government and its reactionary adherents but also broad elements of the political opposition, bureaucratic immobility and suspicion, the conservative and cautious Third and Fourth Dumas—all sufficed to prevent positive reforms in Russian Poland. The ultimate and tragic historical irony of the Russian Empire is that it entered its final agony in 1914 in support of fellow Slavs in the Balkans without having been willing or able to confront its own major Slavic problem.

BIBLIOGRAPHY

PRIMARY SOURCES

Bobrinskii, A. A. "Dnevnik (1910–1911 gg.)," *Krasnyi arkhiv*, 26 (1928), 127–50.
Bok, M. P. *Vospominaniia o moem ottse P. A. Stolypine.* New York, 1953.
"Chronicle," *The Russian Review*, London, 1912–1914.
Dmowski, Roman. *Niemcy, Rosja, i kwestja polska.* Często-chowa, 1938.
———. *Polityka polska i odbudowanie państwa.* 2nd ed. Warsaw, 1926.
Golder, Frank, ed., *Documents of Russian History, 1914–1917.* New York, 1927.
Golovin, F. A. "Zapiski," *Krasnyi arkhiv*, 19 (1926), 110–49.
Gosudarstvennaia deiatel'nost' predsedatelia soveta ministrov stats-sekretaria Petra Arkadevicha Stolypina. 3 parts. St. Petersburg, 1911.
Gosudarstvennaia Duma.
Doklady biudzhetnoi kommissii po razsmotreniiu proekta gosudarstvennoi rospisi, dokhodov i raskhodov. St. Petersburg, 1907–1916.
Obzor deiatel'nosti gosudarstvennoi Dumy tret'iago sozyva, 1907–1912 gg. 3 vols. St. Petersburg, 1912.

Prilozheniia k stenograficheskim otchetam gosudarstven-noi Dumy. 40 vols. St. Petersburg, 1907–1916.

Sbornik materialov. Vtoroi sozyv 1907 god. St. Petersburg, 1907.

Stenograficheskie otchety. Sozyvy I, II, III, IV. 36 vols. St. Petersburg, 1906–1917.

Gosudarstvennyi Sovet. Stenograficheskie otchety. 13 vols. St. Petersburg, 1906–1917.

Guchkov, A. I. "Iz vospominanii A. I. Guchkova," *Poslednia novosti.* Paris, 1936.

————. *Rechi po voprosam gosudarstvennoi oborony i ob obshchei politike 1908–1917.* Petrograd, 1917.

Ivanovich, V. *Rossiiskie partii, soiuzy i ligi. Sbornik ustavov, programm i spravochnykh svedenii.* St. Petersburg, 1906.

Kalinychev, F. I. *Gosudarstvennaia Duma v Rossii v dokumentakh i materialakh.* Moscow, 1957.

Kholmskii vopros. Obzor russkoi periodicheskoi pechati s 1 Jan. 1909 po 1 Jan. 1912. St. Petersburg, 1913.

"Khronika," *Vestnik Evropy.* St. Petersburg, 1907–1914.

Kokovtsov, V. N. *Iz moego proshlago: Vospominaniia 1903–1919.* 2 vols. Paris, 1933.

Korwin-Milewski, H. *Siedemdziesiąt lat wspomnień (1855–1925).* Poznań, 1930.

"Kronika miesięczna." *Biblioteka Warszawska,* Warsaw, 1905–1914.

Krytyka, Kraków, 1905–1914.

Kryzhanovskii, S. E. *Vospominaniia.* Berlin, 1938.

Lazarevskii, N. I. *Zakonodatel'nye akty perekhodnago vremeni 1904–1908 gg.* 3rd ed. St. Petersburg, 1909.

Lednicki, Wacław. *Pamiętniki.* Vol. 2. London, 1967.

Miliukov, P. N. *God bor'by. Publitsisticheskaia khronika 1905–1906.* St. Petersburg, 1907.

————. *Vospominaniia (1859–1917).* 2 vols. New York, 1955.

————. *Vtoraia Duma. Publitsisticheskaia khronika 1907.* St. Petersburg, 1908.

Novoe vremia, St. Petersburg, 1905–1914.

Osvobozhdenie, Paris, 1905.

Padenie tsar'skogo rezhima. 7 vols. Moscow-Leningrad, 1924–1927.

Pares, Bernard. *My Russian Memoirs.* London, 1931.

Pobóg-Malinowski, Władysław. *Narodowa Demokracja 1887–1918. Fakty i dokumenty.* Warsaw, 1933.

Rech', St. Petersburg, 1906–1914.

Rocznik statystyczny Królestwa Polskiego. Rok 1915. Warsaw, 1916.

Russkaia mysl', St. Petersburg, 1907–1914.

Stanowisko stronnictwa demokratyczno-narodowego w chwili obecnej. Warsaw, 1906.

Tret'ia gosudarstvennaia Duma. Materialy dlia otsenki ee deiatel'nosti. St. Petersburg, 1912.

Witte, S. Iu. *Vospominaniia.* 3 vols. Moscow, 1960.

Zakrzewski, A. *Materialy k voprosu ob obrazovanii Kholmskoi gubernii.* Warsaw, 1908.

Zamyslovskii, G. G. *Pol'skii vopros v gosudarstvennoi Dume 3-go sozyva, 1-i sessii.* Vilno, 1909.

SECONDARY SOURCES

Amburger, Erik. *Geschichte der Behördenorganisation Russlands von Peter dem Gossen bis 1917.* Leiden, 1966.

Ammann, Albert M. *Abriss der ostslawischen Kirchengeschichte.* Vienna, 1950.

Arseniev, K., "Khronika," *Vestnik Evropy* (June 1914), pp. 350–51.

Avrekh, A. Ia. *Stolypin i tret'ia Duma.* Moscow, 1968.

————. *Tsarizm i tret'eiiunskaia sistema.* Moscow, 1966.

————. "Vopros o zapadnom zemstve i bankrotstvo Stolypina," *Istoricheskie zapiski*, 70 (1961), 61–112.

Bazylow, Ludwik. *Polityka wewnętrzna caratu i ruchy społeczne w Rosji na początku XX wieku*. Warsaw, 1966.

————. "Problemy narodowościowe w politycznym życiu Rosji po rewolucji 1905 r.," *Naród i Państwo. Prace ofiarowane Henrykowi Jabłońskiemu w 60 rocznicę urodzin*. Warsaw, 1969. Pp. 25–35.

Belokonskii, I. P. *Zemskoe dvizhenie*. 2nd ed. Moscow, 1914.

Bulat, Wojciech. "Zjazd polsko-rosyjski w Moskwie 21–22 kwietnia 1905 roku," *Studia z najnowszych dziejów powszechnych*, 2 (1962), 187–208.

Charques, Richard. *The Twilight of Imperial Russia*. London, 1965.

Chmielewski, Edward. "Stolypin's Last Crisis," *California Slavic Studies*, 3 (1964), 95–126.

————. "Stolypin and the Russian Ministerial Crisis of 1909," *California Slavic Studies*, 4 (1967), 1–38.

Clemens, I. "Pol'sha," *Ezhegodnik gazety Rech' na 1914 god*. St. Petersburg, 1914. Pp. 249–67.

"The Country of Chełm," *Polish Encyclopedia*. Geneva, 1925. Vol. 2. Pp. 722–49.

Dallin, Alexander, "The Future of Poland," *Russian Diplomacy and Eastern Europe, 1914–1917*. New York, 1963. Pp. 1–77.

Dymsza, L. *La question de Khelm*. Paris, 1911.

Feldman, Wilhelm. *Dzieje polskiej myśli politycznej 1864–1914*. 2nd ed. Warsaw, 1933.

Fleischhacker, Hedwig, *Russische Antworten auf die polnische Frage, 1795–1917*. Berlin, 1941.

Gargas, Sigismund. "Die Chelmer Frage," *Die Kultur*, 3 (1912), 313–31.

Gorin, P. "Natsional'naia politika tsarizma v Pol'she v XX veke," *Bor'ba klassov*, 10 (1933), 63–69.

Halecki, O. *Polens Ostgrenze im Lichte der Geschichte Ostgaliziens, des Chelmer Landes und Podlachiens*. Vienna, 1918.

Harper, Samuel N. *The New Electoral Law for the Russian Duma*. Chicago, 1908.

Hoetzsch, Otto. *Russland. Eine Einführung auf Grund seiner Geschichte vom Japanischen bis zum Weltkrieg*. 2nd ed. Berlin, 1917.

Izgoev, A. S. "Ot tret'ei Dumy k chetvertoi," *Ezhegodnik gazety Rech' na 1913 god*. St. Petersburg, 1913. Pp. 186–97.

————. "Politicheskaia zhizn' v Rossii," *Russkaia mysl'* (April 1911), pp. 3–4; (January 1912), p. 5.

————. *P. A. Stolypin. Ocherk zhizni i deiatel'nosti*. Moscow, 1912.

Kieniewicz, Stefan. *Historia Polski 1795–1918*. Warsaw, 1968.

Kornilov, A. A. *Russkaia politika v Pol'she so vremeni razdelov do nachala XX veka*. Petrograd, 1915.

Kukiel, Marian. *Dzieje Polski porozbiorowe*. London, 1961.

Lednicki, Aleksander, "P. N. Miliukov i pol'skii vopros," *P. N. Miliukov: sbornik materialov po chestvovaniiu ego semidesiatiletiia 1859–1929*, ed. S. A. Smirnov et al. Paris, 1929. Pp. 212–217.

Lednicki, Wacław, "Rosyjsko-polska Entente Cordiale: jej początki i fundamenty 1903–1905," *Zeszyty Historyczne*, 10 (1966), 9–142.

Levin, Alfred. "June 3, 1907: Action and Reaction," *Essays in Russian History*, ed. Alan D. Ferguson and Alfred Levin. Hamden, Conn. 1964. Pp. 231–73.

————. *The Second Duma*. New Haven, 1940.

Łukawski, Zygmunt. *Koło polskie w rosyjskiej dumie państwowej w latach 1906–1909.* Wrocław, 1967.

————. "Rosyjskie ugrupowania polityczne wobec sprawy autonomii Królestwa Polskiego w okresie 1905–1917 (W świetle archiwalnych materiałów rosyjskich)," *Zeszyty naukowe Uniwersytetu Jagiellońskiego. Prace historyczne,* 9 (1962), 145–70.

Marchand, René. *Les grands problèmes de la politique intérieure russe.* Paris, 1912.

Martov, L., Maslov, P., Potresov, A., eds. *Obshchestvennoe dvizhenie v Rossii v nachale XX-go veka.* 4 vols. in 6. St. Petersburg, 1909–1914.

Miketov, Ia. *Chto sdelalo narodnoe predstaviteľstvo treťiago sozyva.* St. Petersburg, 1912.

Miliukov, Paul. "Aleksander Lednicki jako rzecznik polskorosyjskiego porozumienia," *Przegląd współczesny,* 3 (1939), 25–71.

Miliukov, P. N. "Politicheskie partii v gosudarstvennoi Dume za piat' let," *Ezhegodnik gazety Rech' na 1912 god.* St. Petersburg, 1912. Pp. 77–96.

Nagórski, Zygmunt. "Aleksander Lednicki (1866–1934)," *Zeszyty Historyczne,* 1, (1962), 27–66.

Pobóg-Malinowski, Władysław. *Najnowsza historia polityczna Polski.* Vol. I, 2nd ed., 2 vols., London, 1963–1967.

Pogodin, A. L. *Glavnye techeniia poľskoi politicheskoi mysli (1863–1907).* St. Petersburg, 1907.

Polejaieff, Pierre. *Six Années. La Russie de 1906 à 1912.* Paris, 1912.

Savickij, Nicolas. "P. A. Stolypin," *Le Monde slave,* 4 (Nov. 1933), 227–63.

Shingarev, A. "Zemskoe i gorodskoe samoupravlenie," *Ezhegodnik gazety Rech' na 1914 god.* St. Petersburg, 1914. Pp. 216–40.

Sidel'nikov, S. M. *Obrazovanie i deiatel'nost' pervoi gosu-darstvennoi Dumy.* Moscow, 1962.

Siemieński, Józef, ed. *La Pologne. Son histoire, son organi-sation et sa vie.* Lausanne-Paris, 1918.

Smith, C. Jay. "The Russian Third State Duma: An Analyti-cal Profile," *Russian Review,* 17 (July 1958), 201–10.

Stakhovich, A. "Kholmskii vopros," *Russkaia mysl'* (Feb. 1911), pp. 74–95; (March 1911), pp. 87–105.

Staszyński, Edmund. *Polityka oświatowa caratu w Królest-wie Polskim. Od powstania styczniowego do I wojny światowej.* Warsaw, 1968.

Stepanskii, A. D. "Politicheskie gruppirovki v gosudarstven-nom Sovete v 1906–1907 gg.," *Istoriia SSSR,* 4 (1965), 49–65.

Trutovskii, Vladimir. *Sovremennoe zemstvo.* Petrograd, 1914.

Veselovskii, Boris. *Istoriia zemstva.* Vol. 3. St. Petersburg, 1911.

"Vybory," *Ezhegodnik gazety Rech' na 1913 god.* St. Peters-burg, 1913. Pp. 198–239.

Walsh, W. B. "The Composition of the Dumas," *Russian Review,* 8 (April 1949), 111–16.

Wasilewski, Leon. *Chełmszczyzna i sprawa jej oderwania.* Kraków, 1913.

———. *Der Kampf um das Chelmerland.* Vienna, 1919.

———. *Die Ostprovinzen des alten Polenreichs.* Kraków, 1916.

———. *Dzieje męczeńskie Podlasia i Chełmszczyzny.* 2nd ed. Kraków, 1918.

———. *La paix avec l'Ukraine.* Geneva, 1918.

———. *Rosja wobec Polaków w dobie "konstitucyjnej."* Kraków, 1916.

————. *Rosyjskie partye polityczne i ich stosunek do sprawy polskiej*. Kraków, 1905.

Wiercieński, Henryk. *Ziemia Chełmska i Podlasie. Rys historyczny i obraz stanu dzisiejszego*. Warsaw, 1919.

Wierzchowski, Mirosław. "Problematyka polska w rosyjskiej prasie liberalnej w latach 1907–1912," *Studia z dziejów ZSRR i krajów Europy Środkowej*, 1 (1965), 164–95.

————. "Sprawa Chełmszczyzny w rosyjskiej Dumie Państwowej," *Przegląd Historyczny*, 1 (1966), 97–123.

————. "Sprawa polska w programach i taktyce rosyjskich partii politycznych w latach 1905–1914," *Studia z dziejów ZSRR i Europy Środkowej*, 2 (1967), 81–99.

————. *Sprawy Polski w III i IV Dumie Państwowej*. Warsaw, 1966.

————. "Sprawy polskie w III Dumie państwowej (1907–1912)," *Kwartalnik Historyczny*, 2 (1963), 405–26.

Winter, Edward. *Russland und das Papsttum*. Vol. 2. Berlin, 1961.

INDEX

Index

Maciejewicz, Stanisław, 70
Makarov, A. A., 40, 52, 126–27, 133
Maklakov, N. A., 155
Maklakov, V. A., 130
Manifesto of June 3, 1907, 43–44, 53, 58, 172
Markov, N. E., 47, 64, 75, 127, 145
Maslennikov, A. M., 151
Meysztowicz, Aleksander, 101, 133
Mickiewicz, Adam, 18
Miliukov, P. N., 27, 34–35, 39, 45, 64, 78, 96, 134, 165–66, 172
Miliutin, N. A., 112–13
Minsk, 23n, 84, 103
Moderate Rightists, 45, 47, 54–55, 61, 84
Mogilev, 23n, 84–85
Mother of Polish Schools, 24
Münchengrätz, 10
Municipal Regulations of 1892, 138–41, 146–47, 149, 151, 154, 156
Muraviev, M. N., 17
Muraviev, N. V., 114
Muromtsev, S. A., 40

Napoleon III, 11
Napoleonic Code, 8, 15, 120, 124, 129, 133
Naryshkin, A. A., 148
National Democrats, 20–21, 25, 33, 37, 44
National League, 20
Neidhardt, A. B., 100
Nicholas I, 6–7, 10, 34
Nicholas II, 18, 21–22, 60, 108–109
Nicholas, Grand Duke, 168
Novoe vremia, 39–40, 59, 104
Novosiltsev, N. N., 5

Obolenskii, A. D., 101
October Manifesto of 1905, 21, 24, 121, 125
Octobrists, 29, 31, 35, 39, 45, 50, 52, 54–55, 57–63, 65–66, 76–78, 84, 88, 94, 98, 109–10, 125, 129, 131, 133–34, 143, 145, 157, 160–62, 165, 172
Opole church question, 66–68, 95

Organic Statute of 1832, 8, 34
Orlov, A. F., 11

Papacy, 10, 16
Parczewski, Alfons, 73
Paskevich, I. F., 8, 10–11
Patriotic Society, 6
Peasants, emancipation of, 13–14
Pikhno, D. I., 84, 132–33
Pius IX, Pope, 16
Pobedonostsev, K. P., 112–14, 117
Podlasie, 111
Podolia, 18, 23n, 84
Pokrovskii, I. P., 80, 97
Polish League, 19
Potulov, V. A., 129
Progressives, 45, 65, 129, 145–46
Prussia, 10, 19, 167
Purishkevich, V. M., 47–48, 54, 64, 81, 163
Pushkin, Alexander, 8

Rech', 35, 59
Religion, instruction of in schools in Poland, 23–24
Revolution of 1905, 128, 159, 172
Rightists in the State Duma, 45, 47, 54, 61, 63–65, 68, 77, 93–94, 123–24, 127, 129, 133, 157–58, 173
Rodichev, F. I., 28, 56–57, 67, 96, 129, 131–32, 151–53
Roman Catholic Church, 16–17, 23, 66–67, 86–87, 112, 114, 116, 118, 120–24, 128
Rotwand, Stanisław, 132
Russian Nationalist party, 45, 61, 71, 81–83, 94, 98, 123–24, 126, 129, 133, 135–37, 157, 160, 173
Russian Orthodox Church, 10, 16, 23, 38, 57, 88–89, 92, 94, 98, 106, 112–14, 116, 120–24, 131, 150, 163
Russo-Japanese War, 20–21
Rząd, Antoni, 55

Sazonov, S. D., 158, 173
Schools, elementary, in Poland, 24, 36, 40, 50, 55–56, 68–72, 160
Schools, higher elementary, in Poland, 72–74

Index

Wiercieński, Henryk, 112
Witte, S. Iu., 25, 51–52, 83–84, 99–101, 103, 114, 123

Zajączek, Józef, 5
Zamość, 121
Zamoyski, Andrzej, 11–12
Zamyslovskii, G. G., 47–48, 62, 157–58

Zemstvos, 30, 32–33, 55–56, 64, 76–78, 83, 86, 99–100. *See also* Western zemstvos
Zhitomir, 120, 129
Zinoviev, N. A., 101–102, 146, 148, 155
Żukowski, Władysław, 42, 63, 65, 79–81
Zurabov, A. G., 42

The Polish Question has been set on the Linotype in eleven point Caledonia with two-point line spacing. Weiss Series I was selected for display. The book was designed by Jim Billingsley, composed and printed by Heritage Printers, Inc., Charlotte, North Carolina, and bound by the Becktold Company, St. Louis, Missouri. The paper on which the book is printed is designed for an effective life of at least three hundred years.

THE UNIVERSITY OF TENNESSEE PRESS